ROLLING THUNDER
SPEAKS

ROLLING THUNDER SPEAKS

A Message for Turtle Island

ROLLING THUNDER

Edited by
CARMEN SUN RISING POPE

Clear Light Publishers
Santa Fe, New Mexico

Dedication

This book is dedicated to Steven Brokenfoot Cook,
who took me out into the hills that day
to help me find my vision.

© 1999 by Carmen Sun Rising Pope
Clear Light Publishers, 823 Don Diego, Santa Fe, NM 87501
WEB SITE: www.clearlightbooks.com

Library of Congress Cataloging-in-Publication Data
Rolling Thunder.
    Rolling Thunder speaks : a message for Turtle Island / edited
by Carmen Sun Rising Pope.
    p.   cm.
    ISBN 1-57416-026-5 (alk. paper)
    1. Rolling Thunder. 2. Indians of North America—Medicine.
3. Indians of North America—Religion.   4. Indians of North
America—Biography.   5. Cherokee Indians—Biography.
I. Pope, Carmen Sun Rising.   II. Title
E90.R74R65   1999
299'.7—dc21   99–12791
                                                                    CIP

First Edition
10 9 8 7 6 5 4 3 2

Photographs © by Carmen Sun Rising Pope
Book Interior Design/Production by Vicki S. Elliott
Printed in Canada

DISCLAIMER: No advice, herbal treatments, or remedies
provided in this book are intended to
replace qualified medical advice from a
licensed physician.

Contents

Acknowledgments

My love and appreciation go to these Thunder People who
supported me during the past year and made it possible
for this book to be written.

Barbara Simeroth, my chief and my sister
Bradley Geronimo Urbanski, who understands respect
Craig Fitch, who never told me what to do
Danny Lumer, who always had a big smile
Dr. David Brooks, a true Christian saint
Delilah Coyote Singing, who never lost faith
Derek Broken Canoe, my hunka nephew
Don Hines, who never questioned my path
Gadohi Usquanigodi, who fixed my car, again and again
Imelda Sharp, who never wrote
Jesse Black Wolf, who chopped wood to keep me warm
Jim Rowland, a special pen pal
Kozue Okada, a gentle spirit from Japan
Masatake Aoyama, who built a fence
Mike Kamen, my smoking mirror
Norimoto Yoshida, a small man with a big heart
Paul and Chris Norman, who paid the bills so I could write
Rick, Toni, and Amy Childers, who made it possible
  to move to the camp
Tom Sherratt, our beloved Uncle
Rolling Thunder, who held my hand through it all
And Grandfather Great Spirit, who patiently nudged me along
                                        —Carmen Sun Rising Pope

Foreword

By Sun Rising Pope

Rolling Thunder was born of the Paint Clan of the Cherokees, the clan of the medicine people. His paternal grandfather was a traditional chief and medicine man, who was murdered by tribal police when Rolling Thunder's father was a young child. So it was that RT (as he is known to his friends) entered his third reincarnation with a legacy of great spiritual power, leadership, and history of genocide against his race.

This legacy set the tone for RT's entire life. There was nothing ordinary about him or his life, from his training to the medicine trail at a young age, to riding the trains as a hobo during the Depression, to the creation—literally from the sagebrush up—of his traditional Indian camp, Meta Tantay. Rolling Thunder was a remarkable individual who touched the lives of thousands of people across all cultures and races during his eighty-year walk on this earth.

RT was not a Cherokee medicine man. He did not live on a Cherokee reservation nor study solely the Cherokee medicine path. The correct designation would be intertribal medicine man as his teachers included Gray Horse of the Paiutes, Frank Fool's Crow of the Sioux, and Mad Bear Anderson of the Tuscarora. Likewise, he did not minister to only Native Americans. He healed many people of all races.

As a young man living in California, he was active working with the Chumash, Miwok, and other California tribes in their fight to retain their lands, rights, and sovereignty. He came to Nevada in his early thirties to study Shoshone medicine, and immediately became involved in the Western Shoshone legal battles to hold the U.S. government accountable to the conditions of the Treaty of Ruby Valley. More than just spearheading the Western Shoshone land fight, he was also instrumental in reawakening the pride and spirit of the Western Shoshone. I've been told that he was the person who revived the "fandangos" on the Duckwater and South Fork reservations.

For those of us who believe that way, the Sixties began a major shift in the American consciousness due to a particular alignment of celestial bodies. It was time for the messengers, and time for traditionals to openly share their knowledge with non-Natives. This decade began a shift in focus for RT from Native land issues to traveling among non-Natives, carrying the message and seeking brothers and sisters of all colors from all walks of life.

It was during this time that RT made his Grateful Dead connection and initiated a connection with the young hippies that would last until hippies were replaced by yuppies. Mickey Hart produced the Rolling Thunder album, which opens with RT giving his traditional invocation. Jerry Garcia produced Uncle John's Band, a tribute to RT, whose white name is John Pope. Bob Dylan led the Rolling Thunder Revue, and Tom Laughlin starred in the Billy Jack movies, which were based on true incidents in RT's life.

The Seventies were a time of very public life for RT. Beginning with his historic talk for the Menninger Foundation in Kansas to his trip to the United Nations with Grandfather David Monongye and his appearance at the World Symposium on Humanity in Vancouver, he traveled throughout the United States, Canada, and Europe sharing his message for the brotherhood of mankind. He spoke at the Cayce Foundation in Virginia, the University of Texas at Austin, the Indian Center in Vancouver, the University of California at Berkeley, in Yakatat, Alaska, and in Denmark and Austria, to name just a few. And the thunder and the lightning accompanied him all along the way.

He was interviewed by *Mother Earth* magazine, *Shaman's Drum,* the *National Enquirer* and every local newspaper in the towns where he spoke. As a spiritual reawakening began to take hold throughout the world, more and more people were open and interested in what Indians had to say and share. Authors referenced him in their works. People began to seek him out for healing, for instruction. He could not be ignored. Even the U.S. government acknowledged him by its presence at his talks and during his tours.

As with all things, there were negative repercussions to this fame. He was controversial, he was criticized by Natives and non-Natives alike. He never minced his words nor backed away from unpopular issues. Death threats were made by groups of all colors and the everpresent CIA man shadowed his movements. During the siege at Wounded Knee, South Dakota, his home in Carlin, Nevada, was surrounded by federal troops. And then there was always the danger of bad medicine sent to him by those whose spiritual talents were manipulated by evil.

By the end of the Seventies his dream of building a traditional Indian community based on living in harmony with nature rather than the delusion of conquering it became a reality. After purchasing 262 acres outside of Carlin's city limits, he began Meta Tantay. People from all over the world and every background imaginable came to visit Meta Tantay. Buckminster Fuller, the Grateful Dead, Tibetan monks, and young street people found their way there. Some stayed, and others came just to see how the community operated. All left with something more in their hearts and spirits than when they arrived.

In the early part of the Eighties, the camp was growing and the desert was blossoming, but it wasn't meant to be at that time. Some have said the camp was twenty years ahead of its time. Some have said such a community just isn't feasible in this day and age. I think only RT and the Great Spirit know the real reason the camp fissured, broke apart, and finally dissipated.

The health of both RT and his beloved wife of forty years, Spotted Fawn, began to fail. When Spotted Fawn crossed over to the other side, RT withdrew physically and emotionally from the camp. He began drinking, which aggravated his diabetes and heart condition. As he withdrew from people, many of his friends also withdrew, unable to watch the anger and feel the pain that was so evident in RT's life during that time. By the summer of 1989, RT had lost a leg due to diabetes and was confined to a wheelchair.

Since his health prevented him from traveling, people continued to come to the tiny town of Carlin to honor and learn from him. Although he claimed that he had retired from healing, he never turned down a sincere request. Even though such healing work taxed him severely physically, he continued to give of himself as he had all his life.

Heart attacks became more frequent. Emphysema forced him to become attached nearly 24 hours a day to a portable air tank. Each successive health crisis brought him closer and closer to the other side. Friends began suggesting, then admonishing, and finally begging him to write the book that he had been talking about since 1982. Once he was gone, so too would his wisdom, his knowledge, and his message be lost to those he left behind.

Over the years, many people approached him about collaborating with him on a book. I don't know why it never happened. RT would say because it was not meant to be at that time. I myself came to Carlin after talking with RT by telephone with delusions of working with him on his book. Once I arrived and became fully enmeshed in the (to my eyes) chaotic situation, I quickly dismissed fancy notions of writing a book with Rolling Thunder. There was just too much housework, office work, garden work, and caretaking for there to ever be time to work on a book.

By late November 1996, RT knew that his time was almost up. That knowledge was confirmed for me when in early December 1996 he agreed to have an unpublished author from the east coast write the story of his life. At last RT seemed serious about getting a book written, and I knew it would be his last project. It was a bittersweet moment, and for a time we both tried to act like nothing was out of the ordinary. But delusions are frail creations. Labored breathing, even with oxygen, and gangrene exposing bone could not be ignored.

RT recorded tapes of his life's story but he was dissatisfied with the book proposal. "I'm not really looking for someone to write about me," he said. "I'm looking for someone to write about the Great Spirit." By the end of December he was adamant. "Don't send him any more tapes. We'll find someone else to write the book," he told me. As usual, I disobeyed him. I couldn't see how this person was not working out and felt that RT was being unreasonable. I continued to make copies of RT's talks and send them to the east coast. In my foolish arrogance, I forgot that RT could "see" in a way that I could not.

In the early morning of January 23, 1997, Grandmother Moon showed her full light over a foot of fresh snow and RT crossed over to the spirit world. For one precious hour all was peaceful and calm, and I could pretend that he was just sleeping and would waken at any minute and call me to his room. I took sixty minutes to hold onto my world as I had known it for the last three years before the foggy haze of intense pain hit and an uncomprehending daze came over me.

It was sometime during this blurred part of my life that I made the decision to revoke permission to the east coast writer to write RT's book. There were numerous phone calls from him with requests becoming more and more disrespectful. When he asked me to send him RT's turban so he could wear it and "get in touch with RT's spirit" to help him write the book, alarm bells that had been quietly but insistently ringing for some time began to develop into a crescendo. Finally, in April 1997, when he sent me a taped session he had with a channeler who claimed to channel RT's spirit, outrage and indignation cut through the fog enveloping me and I revoked permission for him to write the book.

That decision left me in a quandary. Who should write this book? I didn't know any authors or have any connections with the publishing industry. I went to friends for advice. Mostly they were silent. Their silence didn't register with me and I kept asking. Slowly a feeling was growing inside me that maybe I could write the book. After all, it was basically recorded on tape and just needed to be transcribed and organized a little. That thought was terrifying to me so I buried it as deeply as I could, but it continued to resurrect itself until I could no longer easily ignore it.

It was during this time, toward the end of April, that Steve Brokenfoot Cook, a friend of ours, came to visit. I will always be indebted to Steve for what he did for me that day. Although there was tons of work that needed to be done at the house, we both felt pulled by Spirit to drive out into the foothills around Carlin and visit what I call the Secret, Hidden Magic Valley—for that is what it is. It is a place where the veil of the physical world is thin and the spirit world easily accessible. After spending the entire day in the hills, we returned to the house for dinner, herbal tea, and quiet, reflective conversation.

Steve brought up the subject of RT's book. He asked about my thoughts about who to commission to write it. I think because the entire day had been spent in such a spiritual place and because I was at peace for the first time in months, I felt safe enough to tell Steve that for a while I'd been getting the feeling that maybe I should write it. It was a delicate moment for me because if I had sensed any negative judgment from Steve, despite anything positive he might say, the idea would have retreated into my psyche never to be found again. That is why this book is dedicated to Steve Brokenfoot Cook. His reaction was so genuine, so positive, that it gave me the courage to go forward and act on my idea. Thank you, Steve.

And so, after months of transcribing tapes, reviewing RT's writings and notes, and remembering stories and lessons, RT's dream of his own book in his own words has taken form. This book is a compilation of Rolling Thunder's talks, writings, and dining room discussions that span a period of thirty years. The words are his words; nothing is in this book that RT did not teach. The book is him, speaking in his own style, informing, admonishing, and offering solutions. It is his gift of love to you and to me. *Aho.*

Introduction
By Rolling Thunder

Some people tell me that a man named Doug Boyd wrote a book about me. I don't have much time to read, so I've never read it. Some of my family read it and they say it's okay, but I think it's getting kind of outdated. Fact is, I'm working on the next book. I'm tired of white people writing about us, that we walked across the Bering Strait and that kind of junk. So I'm writing it, and I work on my own terms. I've helped make four moving pictures, and it has to be real, whatever I do, and then I only put out so much. I don't pull any punches and I don't work for anyone except the Grandfather Great Spirit. I know my English is poor, but still, I've already got somebody picked, a young Indian who's educated, to help me straighten out some of it, and at least take out the swear words.

I want a book that's gonna be heavier than any written yet, so you might prepare yourself because I'm going to hit you with a lot of truths. It'll be from the inside looking out. The other one that Doug Boyd wrote was from the outside looking in. I can't say when or how, but I'll tell you one thing, it's going to be factual and it's going to tell the truth. It's gonna be real and it's gonna be original.

It'll be about some of the ancient civilizations, things that people seem to be interested in, but that's not all. It'll also be about what's been going on and how people in "civilized societies" got themselves into conditions where they are already on the way down. It'll be about what happened to the ancient ones and how they went down, some prophecies, and how it'll be in the future. In other words, it'll have to cover quite a bit. I want to write about things all people can benefit from: how we can have peace in the world and how we can clean up the pollution. I like to show the reasons why it doesn't have to be that way, and what the solutions could be. I don't think people are getting good answers these days from their politicians, governments, and their own religions.

—1982

CHAPTER ONE

Rolling Thunder, circa 1930.

Rolling Thunder on speaking tour in United States, 1976.

The Medicine Trail

"I don't like to talk too much about what I can do by myself. I tell people I don't do anything, that it is the Great Spirit's power."

Origins of a Medicine Man

My name is Rolling Thunder and I was born to be a medicine man. People ask me, "How do you know if you're meant to be a medicine man?" You just know if it's meant to be, or at least you do if you're an Indian. It's partly instinct and partly a search for your purpose in life.

There were lots of signs when I was young that I was going to be a medicine man. There are certain marks on the body, certain signs; the elders examine the baby when it's born and they have a way of knowing. Sometimes the mother or father of a person born to be a medicine man will have a vision, and the child will get his name before he is born. When a person is named in this way before he's born, that's a sure sign that he's supposed to be a medicine man.

Medicine men get their names in many ways; it isn't a routine thing. My name has two meanings: "Walking with the Truth" and "Song to the Gods." They tell me that before I could talk, when I was just a baby in diapers, I used to run out into the storm and scream like a little eagle. I'd dance and holler with the thunder rolling overhead and the lightning flashing all around me. I love the storms and always have, and I relate very closely to both thunder and lightning.

When I was a young boy, my family lived outside of Big Cedar, Oklahoma, in a tent that leaked when it rained. When I was about five years old, my folks wanted to be alone so they sent me to the post office. I'd been there before, but with big people, never alone. On the way to the post office I felt very lonely, but I had a deep sense that somebody or something was watching me. All at once a big animal jumped out of the woods from behind me. It didn't harm me but ran around and walked in front of me. And we walked together for a time and I wasn't lonely anymore.

The animal was big and yellow and shaggy all around his neck. I thought he was a big shaggy dog, except that when he turned and looked at me I could see he had a face more like a cat's. As we got closer to the town, I heard people yelling and dogs barking. When the animal heard the dogs barking, he stopped and turned his head and looked at me as if to say good-bye, and then he ran off into the brush.

Some people came running over to me and asked me if I had seen a mountain lion. I said no, but that I had seen a big, yellow shaggy dog. I described him and they said it was a mountain lion that they had been trying to find and kill. The people then took me home to my folks and told them what happened. The lion could have harmed me but he did not, didn't offer to. After that my folks never sent me alone to town again.

I was born a Cherokee, but I roamed around from tribe to tribe like most young men do until they find a woman somewhere—maybe of some other tribe—and settle down. I have lived with many different tribes. The medicine man would adopt me as his son and I'd be his helper. Then I'd move on to another tribe. So I got my training by living with different tribes. I came to this area of Nevada because the Shoshoni have some of the most powerful medicines around, and I knew that it would be a good place to learn about the herbs and the medicine. In this area of Nevada, a fault line—a place of natural power—is near-by. This is high desert country, 5,000-foot altitude on the flats. It's high, dry, and cold, but the air is still clean and pure.

Everything that happened in my whole life was part of my training toward becoming a medicine man. I was raised in eastern Oklahoma in a range of the Ozarks called the Kiamichi Mountains, and heard all the stories from my father's side and from some of the old white men's side. I've been told that before I was born, during my father's youth, those hills were Indian territory. But the land was taken away from our tribe and we retreated to the wooded areas to live. I was a youngster during the Depression, so we had to make a living practically with our bare hands, just as our ancestors had done.

I didn't go very far in school, but maybe I went to a different type of school. At about the age of fifteen I built my first house—a log cabin with a smokehouse and a corral for goats and hogs. I lived alone there for quite a while and worked an acre of land with a hoe and shovel. Those were mighty rough times, but they taught me a lot about nature and the ways of living in harmony with Mother Earth.

Later, when I was older, I was always called on to doctor in ceremonies and in other places wherever I'd go. I suppose the first time I understood this was the time I was traveling through the country and felt a strong pull to visit a little Indian ranch in California, even though I had no plan to go there. I had known this highly spiritual old lady and some of the other people who lived there for a long time. She had always been kind to me and my wife. I went to the ranch to visit again, and the old lady was very sick, dying. All the doctors had given up and had left the room. The house was full of her relations.

When I walked in, her relations asked me to do something for her. It seemed like they all knew that I was the one to do this thing, to get her well. She was around eighty years old. The first thing I had them do was to take all the white man's medicine out of the house. Then I sat up with her all night, and they assigned a young lady to help me, kinda like a nurse. All night long I prayed over this old lady.

The blood had left her veins—which had turned purple and stood out. Along toward morning the blood started to come back, and around sunrise she opened her eyes. I was standing at the foot of her bed and she smiled at me. The first thing she said to me was, "Have you eaten?" A real Indian woman. I told her, "No grandmother, I can't eat until you eat."

Her relations came through while the old woman and I were eating. They put their hands on my shoulder and said, "God bless you." The birds came to the window. One of them said, "They are talking our language." Everything was happy, the sun was shining, the birds were there at the window singing, and the old lady got well. It was just something that was meant to be. I never worried about it or pushed for it. And so I learned my destiny through such things in my early life.

Training for the medicine among our people involves twenty to thirty years before you even start to practice. I learned how to forage for nuts, berries, and roots in the forest, and how to catch fish by setting traps in the water. I also taught myself to recognize all the local plants, although I never got to know many of them by their English or Latin names. Instead, I made up my own labels for each one and I learned how to use them for food and medicine.

A person not born to the medicine can be a medicine person too, but it's harder for them. You don't simply read a few textbooks or go to a special school and then start hiring out your services. It doesn't happen that way. People can't simply come to my country, say they want to be a quickie medicine man, and then take a quickie course.

If a person is born to be a medicine man but chooses not to take up the medicine, then he has to have the power removed by another medicine man. Otherwise, the power will turn on him and cause him sickness or bad luck. Choosing not to take up the medicine is not good, but if the person is weak, doesn't have it in him to do it, then it's better to have the power removed.

When a medicine man's time has come, he knows. He may pass his power on to someone to take his place. But if he hasn't found the right person, then he crosses over to the other side and takes his power with him.

The government tried and failed to wipe out all the medicine people. They'd have had to kill all Indians because the medicine is passed down through the bloodlines and at least one child in every seventh generation will be born to the medicine. My own grandfather was a medicine man. So it is that we're still training as many medicine people as we can support.

On Testing and Training

In our way, a person trains for the medicine for twenty to thirty years before he even starts to practice. And there are also rituals to go through where he is very near death each time.

There are seven tests for medicine men, and the purpose of the tests is to earn more power for a good reason. To get more power medicine men have to work for it or make a sacrifice, and some should never go through these tests. Medicine women have their own tests for the same purposes. These tests should be done only under the guidance of someone who is already a highly developed medicine man. There are different levels of spirituality. For example, if a medicine man does something wrong, like making a person sick so he can take money to get him well again, or stealing somebody's wife, he is probably not on a high enough spiritual level to take the tests, much less guide someone.

One of the tests is going alone to a sacred place without a knife or weapon of any kind, but only an eagle feather for protection. The medicine man will spend the night alone in this place. Here he must face his fears. All those things that he fears most will come to him, to frighten him away. To pass this test, he must not run away, but only sit quietly holding his eagle feather, no matter what appears.

Another test involves a mountain of sand. It is very steep, so you have to walk sideways to go up the mountain. Of course, you've had your legs doctored by someone who knows how. When you reach the top of the mountain and you hear a medicine song, it is for you. Do not forget this song as you go down the other side. It is hard to go down because there are steep cliffs, and you cannot see where to step or where the cliffs end. The mountain of sand is like life—it is harder to go down than up.

Another test involves two small trees that look exactly alike. They only get about ten to twelve feet high, and they have berries that look exactly alike. One of the trees has berries that are good to eat, and the berries of the other tree are deadly poison. You stand between the two trees and choose the one that is good to eat. Of course if you fail this test, you don't have to worry about taking it again.

In Shoshone country, a cave is hidden in the Ruby Mountains; a similar place is found in the old Cherokee country of the Smoky Mountains. In this cave lives a huge female snake. She is very poisonous and sometimes aggressive, and it is the same as the rattlesnake with a flat head in Mexico that sometimes grows to as much as twenty feet long. Her name is Achsheba,[1] and she is cared for by those who know. People bring her food and keep a fire going to warm her. She is so huge that she coils herself around the stones of the fire. You have to dance with her and sing your snake song for her. You must walk up to her and begin to sway and dance and sing. She will lift her head to sway back and forth and dance with you. When she opens her mouth and invites you into her jaws, you must put your head in her mouth and lap the saliva from both sides of her tongue. This is the way to please her. If you please her, you tell her your wish and sing her your snake song. Then you withdraw your head, walk away, and do not look back. You can only ask for a wish once, and you can never attempt to return to that place. If you survive, whatever you asked for will be.

Another test involves being shot in the chest. If the person is on a high enough level, the bullets will become molten lead and not harm him.

There are seven of these tests. In all of them the medicine man is very near death. I can never remember all seven of these tests at a time, so I don't think it's meant to be that I should reveal all of them. Certain people might try these things before they are ready, and so they may die because of their ignorance.

Every real medicine person has been to where we are sup-posed to go in the afterlife, or to the place where the evil ones go. Both are only retraining grounds as far as we are concerned. That was my purpose for going to the place where the evil ones go. My intent was not to stay, but as part of the learning pro-cess, to be instructed and to be guided on how to defeat these evil spirits that bother all people and cause much misfortune, including sickness, wars, and destruction. I have also been to the Happy Hunting Ground. Every real medicine person has been there at least once.

The Indian world or the spirit world can be very dan-gerous. I've had people ask me how they can practice astral projection, or travel long distance. Of course it can be done, but why do anything for the sake of curiosity or just because of being greedy or pushy? Such travel is a job for somebody highly trained and for the right reasons. There are certain things I do that I wouldn't ask anyone else to do.

I'd also like to say a word about shapeshifting and making yourself invisible. These things are used in an emergency and for a good purpose. They are never to be used for show or greed, nor should they be used too frequently. I remember a time during the Wounded Knee situation when they were rounding up Indians and throwing us in jail for no good reason. I was with a group of Indians in a parked car. A police-man was coming down the street looking into every car, but when he came to the one we were in, he looked in, shone his flashlight around, but he didn't see us. He just walked right on by and left us in peace. And then there was the time that my sister looked for me all over the reservation, but couldn't see me even though I was there the entire time. Doing these types of things frequently is not a good idea, in part because they may become permanent, and we are not supposed to harm anything or anyone.

I like to test myself once in a while. In other words, if I get a piece of fruit that's green and not ripe, I can hold it in my hands a few minutes after I get used to it and the fruit will ripen while I hold it. The fruit will pass from green to ripe within two or three minutes. I don't think that's any big deal. I've heard of some of the eastern yogis who would make a whole bowl of fruit appear on the table. I knew of one Indian who might be walking along the highway, and a banana might fall out of the sky in front of him if he was hungry. I encourage people to test themselves by seeing how close they can get to a bird before the bird flies away or to an animal before the animal runs from them.

Rolling Thunder's Vision

I have been asked where my healing power comes from. My power to heal, or I should say, the Great Spirit's power of healing, comes from the Grandfather Great Spirit himself, and was given to me during a powerful vision. There was a time many years ago when it seemed that we Indians were declining, and quickly. The young ones were being destroyed by alcohol, the government was taking our land, the Mother Earth was being destroyed by greed. The white man was making war against the trees and the animals.

I threw myself on the ground, on Mother Earth, and cried out against these things. I didn't want anyone to ever see me cry but I couldn't help it. I could do nothing to stop the destruction, and so I prayed to the Mother Earth and Grandfather Great Spirit. I went into a room of my old shack of a house, and my wife saw to it that no one disturbed me. I stayed in that room alone, fasting and praying. I didn't take peyote or anything like it. I prayed and fasted for several days. I had seen into the future, and it seemed as if the white men were going to steal or take Indian lands. I needed more power.

One night while I was on the bed sleeping I was doctored by the Sun God and his helpers. A bright golden light began to shine from one wall of the room. A huge golden door appeared, then opened. Through this door walked the Sun God; a bright golden light shone all around him. He was tall and powerfully built, and he wore a headdress like the one Quetzacóatl wears. I wasn't afraid because I knew he would help me. He walked to the foot of my bed and stood there looking at me. Then his helpers came through the door—warriors with bows and arrows, short like dwarfs, and three stood on each side of my bed. Next came a medicine man. He stood at the foot of the bed too, singing, praying, shaking his rattle over me. He put his hands on me and pressed down. I could feel the bed move and I knew it was real. Evil spirits began to jump out of me. As the evil ones came out of me, the warriors destroyed them with their bows and arrows. After I was purified, an Old One walked through the golden doorway. He was ancient, powerful in mind and body, and very wise. He laid on top of me and pressed down into me hard. He came into me and became a part of me, to give me strength and wisdom.

When I woke up I was crying and felt as if I was on fire. I knew something was different. I had been doctored in a special way from the other world. I felt this great power within me, but I had to learn to live with this tremendous force, to watch every thought or emotion I had twenty-four hours a day. Since the force is so strong, you see, it has a great potential for misuse, and it could really hurt someone if it were used in a negative or destructive way. During the three days after my vision, anyone I touched received a strong shock like electricity. It's difficult for a healer to adjust to such newfound power.

I knew that I had to overcome the angers of the past or I could damage someone close or dear to me. I knew I would have to get over little tempers, emotional stuff. I had to get on a higher level or else I was going to hurt someone. I walked around for weeks with this feeling that the last thing in the world I wanted to do was to hurt someone if they didn't really have it coming, and even then, my mission in life was to try and help people, not hurt them.

Tasks of a Medicine Man

Anyone can have a healing power if it's properly developed, but being a healer doesn't mean a person is a medicine man. Healing is one of a medicine man's jobs, and another is to take care of this Turtle Island according to the laws of this land as given us by the Great Spirit. Wherever the traditional Indians are, there will be those among them who know the laws of the land.

When there are no traditional Indians around—such as in southern Illinois—the land becomes sterile. In these cases there is no one who knows how to take care of the land, and nature gets out of balance. When there are no Indians left in an area, that's when you see cyclones, hurricanes, floods, and droughts. Our job was taken from us by the white man, but we're taking it back.

Another of the medicine man's most important jobs is to see that his people are well fed. In the old times when the Indians would go out on the march to hunting grounds or to collect food supplies, the chiefs and medicine men couldn't eat until all the others had been fed. When everyone was settled in the camp it was different—nothing was too good for the chiefs and medicine people then.

I use my energy to make it rain. I don't relate to the smog in cities, so I bless the rain to settle the smog wherever I go. Then when I leave an area, the rain really comes down. Some folks have tried to accuse me of causing storms and lightning. Well, I relate to it, but no one can control the weather. Medicine men should not do things like calling rain just for the sake of calling rain. I could do it, but I never do things for show. Some of the young ones will attempt to exercise their powers for show once in a while, and then we have floods.

A medicine man then is a spiritual leader. I try to teach people to heal themselves. I'm only one man, and I can't do it all. But if I can teach people to take care of themselves, then I can influence many more people. I have taught people how to put their work lives together with their spiritual lives, and it turns out successful every time. But when people come to me who wish to have a spiritual experience, and they say, "I want this and I want that," then I know they are not ready yet. I'm willing to teach sometimes, but if a person asks me to teach them, that's usually the first sign that they're not ready to learn. I will not send people into something where they might not have a good experience or come out alive—people often try to advance too fast before they clean up their thinking.

Happiness too is the object. That's part of the medicine man's job wherever he goes. A young lady came to our camp and said she thought she was going to see an old decrepit man sitting in a tipi meditating. I don't know where she got that idea. I've met hundreds of medicine men, and some powerful ones among them in Canada and the United States, but I never knew one like that. They were all fully alive and usually pretty healthy themselves. They liked to laugh and joke and have a good time. Indian people like to have a medicine man around because he can bring about a peacefulness and a healing just by being there, even though he's not actually doctoring or putting anything out. We can have a good time just getting people well.

The rule for medicine men is to never go beyond what they know, to be guided by their own wisdom, and to never do anything out of ego or pushiness. I act only as an agent for the Great Spirit; the power comes from the spirit world. We medicine men are just helpers, you might say. I recognize that many people need to be guided, and that's all I am actually—a guide or maybe a teacher. If we medicine men are chosen to be an instrument for Great Spirit's power—in healing, prophecy, or other tasks—then that's all we're supposed to do. We should not take on any authority that we are not delegated.

I've been accused at times of being a pretty mean old man. But there are different ways of getting spiritual experience. I know a lot of people think I'm going to set them out there to meditate somewhere. Well, sometimes fasting and meditating are good for people, but not in all cases. It can be different for each individual according to their knowledge, what they are doing, and what they want to do.

I like to think I'm doing a medicine thing, a healing thing, wherever I see people and shock the hell out of them with the thunder and the lightning, and see them start to wake up and start thinking in good ways. To see their eyes sparkle and start thinking about the good things in this life is a healing. That's why I shock people. If I'm a little rough, it might be because I love people. I like to see them come alive and awaken. If people start thinking in a good way, then they're going to get well, and they'll be better neighbors to the Indian and to all people.

We like people to do things in a correct way, and we medicine men do not have time to fool around. Medicine men are probably the most independent people in the world. If you come to a medicine man sick or needy, he may help you or turn his back and walk away. His actions are determined by whether it was meant to be. Some people are meant to die, and some are meant to get an extension of life. If you have committed a great crime and must pay a penalty, or if your time has run out, medicine men know that these things are not to be interfered with.

Rules for Following the Medicine Trail

We must be humble in the eyes of the Great Spirit. I simply do what is delegated to me. I tell people that I don't do anything, because all power belongs to the Great Spirit, although I may be a channel for the Great Spirit's power.

Traditional people cannot be healers of any kind unless they understand spirituality. Native healers recognize the spirituality of all things that have life, compared to the "civilized" world which often recognizes how much money an item is worth before anything else. Spirituality would be defined as complete peace, perfect balance, and harmony with oneself as well as all living things—two-leggeds, winged ones, and four-leggeds. It means understanding the relatedness of mankind with all other forms of life.

Before you become a healer you must achieve peace of mind, and a spiritual person can make peace. The first requirement for healing is compassion for people, and then comes understanding. These are the things we have to learn within ourselves before we can do anything for someone else that's meant to be or is good. Understanding means that you can actually see into the person to determine what is bothering them, and that you can come up with some answers real fast.

Control of self and overcoming temptation are necessary for great medicine power. For instance, I dropped stick games, the only kind of gambling I ever did. When I started practicing and following the medicine trail, I stopped because I knew people might think I could be tempted to use power to win. If I used my power foolishly, I would run the risk of doctoring someone and it wouldn't work.

Medicine men are taught to avoid doing things, especially medicine, for show or profit. For example, I have never taken a dime in my life for any healing. When I perform a healing I don't touch money. Yet I realize that everybody has to live, but I don't charge any fees. If the patient or patient's family wants to give me a donation for time and trouble and so on, they can put it in an envelope and give it to one of my helpers, and that way I don't have to be bothered with it. I keep my medicine noncommercial and on a high level.

Medicine men don't go around challenging each other unless they are just playing games where nobody gets hurt. They are just little games to prove ourselves and have a little fun, that's all. In other words we might put a stick out in the sagebrush somewhere and the other guy will go out and look for the stick, and then the stick isn't there anymore because it has been moved. Or we might send a dog into the other man's camp just to see what's going on over there and report back to us. That's just normal game playing. We like to have a good laugh and joke. We don't really have contests.

If a medicine man loses a patient, the family of the dead

patient has a right to stone the medicine man to death. So we don't need malpractice insurance. I tell that to my doctor friends and they don't seem to favor it. Also, I never give medicine to others that I don't take first myself. This too is unpopular with my doctor friends.

I resent very much people who hang around me a few days or come to a talk, and then go out and say that he or she is a medicine man or woman. They'd better use those terms carefully or it will come back to them real fast. I think that in the white man's world most people believe that you have to take a course, that you have to force your way into whatever it is you do. This is not the way it is in the spiritual world, or in the Indian world.

You must be born with the potential to be a medicine person, and before you would begin to heal, you study for many years. An example of what can go wrong when a person takes up the medicine too quickly or in the wrong way is a man who claimed he was the rainmaker for the Dalai Lama. He got rain all right. He got floods that washed out Taiwan and killed a lot of people, and so he nearly died. When you take on the responsibility of the medicine power, you better know what you're doing.

No matter how much power you have, you can't force healing. All factors have to come together at the right place and time. Never do anything out of ego or pushiness. What is needed most in healing work is humility before the power of the Great Spirit. We must be humble in the eyes of the Great Spirit. I hear some people refer to the healing power as "my power," but all power comes from the Great Spirit. That's the reason I'm very careful about making any claims, and that's why I tell people I don't do anything.

A medicine man must choose wisely in terms of who to doctor. If I doctor or help someone and they have not earned it, I will pay a price. If this person goes out and commits another wrong, then I am responsible, and it works back on me. Therefore, there are some people no medicine man will touch. The final judgment to help someone is up to the medicine man alone, and he looks into it very carefully.

A lady in Utah that I helped at one time wrote me a letter. She wanted me to take care of her son, who had just returned from Vietnam. According to the young man and his mother, he had machine-gunned a bunch of little children in Vietnam. The other soldiers had given them candy when they passed through, I guess, but when the children ran out to him, he got excited and machine-gunned them. Now the son was going crazy, losing his mind, and she wanted me to take care of him. Anyway, I had to refuse him.

When the woman brought this young man into my house, I was watching him, watching his eyes and every thought he had. When my sons walked into the room with their long hair, headbands, and dark skin, you could see the hatred of this racist redneck she had brought for me to doctor. I told the lady I didn't want to talk to this young man, but I didn't want to turn him down cold. I didn't like his vibrations at all, but I talked to the mother. I told her to have her son return to where the crime was committed and start from there. I said that he wouldn't have to come back to me; medicine people in Native tribes close to nature could be found in Vietnam. I said that when he's ready, he should sit down and have a smoke and think about it, and somebody will come up and tell him where to go. Then he'd come into contact with a medicine person in Vietnam.

But I also told the mother that if her son got himself in order, made atonement for what he'd done first, then there might be a time that I could help him, and that I'd like to help him in spite of his hangups and difficulties. A few days later I got a letter from the lady telling me that her son had made atonement by sending some old clothes to Vietnam and some money to a boys' home over there. That's not what I said at all, and I was sorry to see it happen. But it was a situation that I shouldn't have had anything to do with in the first place. Later I found out that my first judgment of the young man was right. He was trying to get a job as a policeman in Utah and he hated Mexicans, he hated blacks, he hated Indians, and chances are that was the cause of his crime in Vietnam.

On Sickness and Healing

I've said many times that I don't have a license to practice medicine and that I don't practice medicine. Healing is a spiritual thing; I believe in healing the whole being. Most Native healers look much farther than the average doctor, that is, they look to the original cause of a particular illness. All physical trouble begins on the spiritual level.

What's happening in the body isn't the main problem, so true healing requires looking at more than the body. When a modern doctor examines a sick patient, he may see only the illness. If the doctor doesn't understand what the problem really is, then he may prescribe unnecessary things which certainly can't be called healing. Examples are prescribing chemical drugs so that the person won't feel anything, or finding a troubled part of the body, cutting it out, and throwing it in the trash.

Medicine men have to consider the deeper factors in the course of treatment, so we always take many days to look into a case. Every case of sickness or pain is a form of payment of a debt, either for some mistake in the person's past, past life (even back to seven generations), or for a future wrong. In other words, evil spirits can get into a person because they are accepted or welcomed in, and then it becomes physical or mental. The person has done something wrong, and the bad spirits have established themselves in the person. The evil ones have to be eliminated, both internally as well as externally. The evil has to be dealt with from the physical plane as well as the spiritual plane.

Any infection in the body has its roots in a spiritual impurity, but that doesn't mean we're not supposed to do anything to remedy the situation. The medicine man's job is to find out what that debt is and learn how it can be repaid in another, less painful, way. A medicine man may decide not to accept a case if he feels it isn't the correct time for the person to get well. In any event, getting well will not happen unless the person deserves it.

Sometimes a certain sickness or pain should be endured because it's the best possible way to pay the debt involved. If such a pain is made to go away, the price the person pays may become greater in the long run. Anyone who is sick thinks he wants to get well, but the person's spirit knows when it's right or at least necessary to be ill. If the patient is not ready, there is no way any real healer or medicine person can do a thing. Before a person can be doctored, they have to get themselves in order, or the medicine man will have trouble.

MEANS AND WAYS OF HEALING

Many people ask me, "What did you do?" I don't do the same thing every time, and I don't follow a routine. Something comes over me, and if the person is meant to get well, many times I don't remember what I did.

Most medicine men have their own particular methods and equipment, and it's a matter of pride that each one works out an individual routine and doesn't copy anyone else. Of course, a new healer can watch another's way and get some idea of what to do, but the novice gradually develops his personal ritual with his own songs, prayers, and chants.

Sometimes I suck things out of patients with my mouth. The medicine man is not supposed to swallow any of the infection or material that comes out. Other times I use treatments. One of my favorite methods is to use my hands. Say that a man's got a bad back, and he may not even know it. I've found that I can stem my energy in certain ways to make the back come into place. My finger is my knife if I need one, and I can cut off a tree limb or gather my herbs with my finger. So whatever I do is absolutely painless. I also like to use my hands to transfer energy. You see, hands can serve to transmit the energy, the spiritual force, that flows between the two halves of the body, negative and positive.

I believe the healing power has the strength of the Great Spirit, the energy of the thunder and the lightning, and that of all living things. When we speak of the forces of nature, we're speaking about the life force itself, the Great Spirit. The forces of nature are always there; we're never alone. Even the Old Ones gone on are there. I sometimes also ask the stars or the sun to help me or I may call on the great medicine men and tribal chiefs of the past. I tell people my saints are Sitting Bull, Crazy Horse, Geronimo, Quanah Parker, and I call on them when I need help.

Traditional Native healing brings all these forces of life—their power, the thunder, the lightning, animals, and snakes—together as one in order to perform a purification of someone so that they might be free of the sickness or disease that plagues them. Spirituality heals, but not entirely by itself. For a healing one must bring together the spiritual as well as the physical. All things become one.

Peace of mind, and happiness as well, have to be a part of any cure. I put these things all together as one in my mind. There is no room in my mind for any other kind of thought, such as drinking, sex, or whatever. I picture in my mind what's happening after I've looked into the person. That's the kind of power I practice, and I stay with that person until they are healed, no matter how long it takes.

When I do a healing, I tell people I don't do anything myself because there's a great power that comes down around me, into me, and over me. I might *create a condition* for the rain to listen to a prayer, for somebody to come out of prison, or for the Great Spirit to make somebody well. If you have been living right and doing right, the guidance will be provided for you. To choose between good and evil and to choose the right, that's the key to being a spiritual person. We do not practice the kind of medicine that forces people to do things against their will. We want people to be in accord with themselves and all nature. Medicine men don't want to control anyone.

You could almost say Indian healers carry portable x-rays, in that we have a way of looking into people. We're gonna see, feel, and sometimes smell what is bothering a person, and how.

To analyze a person's sickness, we have to be able to see into the person and to discover what originally caused it.

We can see the sickness in some people by the colors around them. The colors around a person who is sick or full of evil thoughts will be black, gray, or a sickly green. Or we might be able to smell the sickness. I have a very intense and powerful sense of smell, and long before a person dies or before they are even sick, I may be able to smell a cancer or something else that doctors' tests may not even show yet. And I can tell how long a person has to live.

I also work with herbs and plants. Plants are helpers and channels for people who are afflicted and need to get well. Herbs can also be used as helpers. I gather my own plants for use in healing ceremonies, but that's not as easy as it sounds. I'm careful about taking anyone along on my herb gathering. I have to know a person pretty well before I can let him come with me. There are all kinds of voices around me that guide me to the plants I need. If someone else is busy asking questions like "what does this herb do," or "what's this one good for," I won't be able to hear and feel the advice given by the spiritual guides. Worse yet, if the person with me is busy and confused in the mind, if they have what I call a "civilized confusion," then the plants I need will be impossible to find, even if they're right at our feet.

My medicine generally comes from herbs, but if no herbs are around, it's possible to make medicine out of water. It's something we learned from the Eskimos, who can take a glass of water and make it boil. It makes a powerful medicine especially if a blade of grass is added.

In Indian medicine, we even doctor with tobacco, externally and internally. But don't try it. Nicotine is very powerful and you might not know the correct dosage. When we take a smoke, we don't smoke from habit. I don't like commercialized cigarettes because of the chemicals, which make smoking habit forming. We use tobacco in rituals and it's good. When I smoke my pipe, it tells me things I need to know. Lots of times I see things that the other person doesn't see inside themselves.

If I sit down to have a smoke, the first thought I have is a good one of friendship, brotherhood, or a wish for someone to get well. Say that I am in the middle of a great city and looking for someone. I might sit down and have a smoke and think about this person, then we seem to come together. When I have a smoke, I might take the direction to move with the spirit and go somewhere where I'm needed.

Sometimes I use songs. They come to me and some of them are very ancient. We call upon the particular forces that are needed, usually by chants and prayers. Prayer is a powerful tool for healing. I believe prayer isn't just a ritual to be observed in church on Sunday. It's a meaningful exercise that should be practiced twenty-four hours a day. Every thought and every word is a prayer. If you look at someone with a hostile thought, a bad thought, you can make that person sick. You can make yourself sick, because your own reflection will come back to you.

Prayer can be used to achieve incredible results. Not long ago when an Indian would shoot a deer with a poisoned arrow, he'd make an offering prayer for that deer. Then he'd cut around the place where the arrow had entered and throw away only that small piece of deer meat. Whatever poison might remain in the deer was then eliminated through the prayer ceremony. In the same way it's possible to pray certain poisons right out of a patient's body.

We also use traditional purification ceremonies which cleanse the body and help maintain good health. In the old days, purification took place through sweat lodges and fasting. Nowadays we sometimes hold purification ceremonies in the local hot springs, where mud soothes the muscles and calms the mind. We have peyote ceremonies where we eat the buttons or drink a tea made from them for purification. Unfortunately, this ritual is often abused by outsiders. The peyote ceremony should not be used to get high or for any other foolishness. We use the herb in a way that we hope will cleanse our bodies and our minds, so we can put ourselves on a higher plane of life.

We sometimes use healing stones that are usually given to us by medicine people. Some we wear around our necks as amulets. We read stones too. I pick up stones sometimes if I'm lost or want to know something. A few old Indians still know how to use crystals like they were used in ancient civilizations. A long time ago I was given a healing crystal by Aminitus Seqouyah, a great medicine man of the Cherokee. I was taken into the woods and shown how to clean it. First, don't use a crystal with a broken point. If the tip is broken off, it's no good. To clean it, which is good to do especially after using it in a healing, you should wash it by holding it in the clean, pure water of a natural mountain creek. This is different from what New Age people do. Then you wrap it up and keep it in the dark, rather than in the sun like some do. These crystals come from deep inside the earth in dark caves, and that's how they like it. Sometimes moonlight is all right for them.

My healing necklace carries my name in picture writing in beadwork and it has a claw holding a crystal that I also use to doctor. There is such a thing as putting life into inanimate objects. I have seen many cases and I have done it myself. Somebody brings me a rock and wants me to hold it for a few minutes to charge it. I've seen small rocks as well as very large and heavy rocks charged by Indians, and sometimes the rocks are hot after being charged. The charging can be done with a crystal, a rock, or any object, even a little piece of wood.

Some say that when I hand the object back to them, they can feel the vibrations. Sometimes they can feel it so that they are charged with a certain kind of good energy. The rocks and metals have life too. If you are powerful enough, you could pick up a rock or crystal and charge it. If you pray over a rock or crystal powerfully enough, it would have healing power.

I use animal and bird helpers in my healings. The eagle feather has a lot of power. We don't kill the big golden eagles native to this country because they are sacred to us. We use their feathers in medicine work. There's more power in my eagle feathers than in my fist, as I was once told by a wise woman. Like everything else in life, eagle feathers can be used for good or bad. You could cut a man's throat with the wing tip feathers, known as the knife or cutting feathers. If you know how, you could perform an operation and remove something that was bothering a person. These feathers can be used to cut out bad spirits or sickness.

My medicine bag is a badger. In it I keep some sacred things I use in medicine: an eagle feather, a horsetail, what you would call a wand from a Zulu medicine man in Africa, and a snake. Snakes are the most sensitive of all creatures and are highly regarded among us. Every animal, every insect, every person has a relationship to a power or powers. I can become an animal or the animal spirit moves into me. I can smell like a wild animal, and I can see like a wild animal. I become one of them, whichever is meant to be, and I guess I make a lot of noise. I might call on any of my helpers. I might call on some of the animal spirits, such as the otter who swims underwater, for people with bad kidneys.

I really got a kick out of it one time when I was going through security at the airport in Anchorage, Alaska. One friendly young lady involved in performing security searches asks me to pull the stuff out of my medicine bag. So I complied. She asks, "What's this?" I said, "Well, that's just a feather fan." "What's this?" "Well, that there's a rattle. It's used for singing and drumming ceremonies." And she says, "What is this?" "Well, I don't know what you'd call it in English but it's used in our rituals."

Then she says, "Have you got anything in the bottom of that medicine bag?" I said, "A snake." And as I reach down to start to pull out the snake, she says, "Oh, no, no, no! You don't need to do that. Go on. Get out of here."

And the poor girl, she wasn't friendly toward me then. I don't know why. At that point I had to figure that if she didn't like my snakes, she didn't like me. So I just went on through. I don't understand "civilized" people sometimes.

I use my mind as well with a purpose. An example in healing is when you can see the person getting well, or in the case of a person with a broken bone, seeing the bones coming together. Sometimes I see people long distance. I might see a big tumor inside their body or something like that just vanishing and going away.

People should first learn patience, compassion, and understanding of themselves, other people, the animals, and all things that have life around them, and to be in accord with all these natural forces. In other words, if you take the first steps yourself, then you are guided. I try always to be guided by the good spirits, not the bad ones. The bad ones have to be put aside at all times. We have to blank the bad ones out in order to bring about any healing and so that we can become stronger.

I go into purification ceremonies with Indian people from time to time and sometimes by myself. Fasting and prayer are among the many ways that we have of developing the healing power. But I do believe and I'd like for people to keep in mind that all ways—even Christian ways or Buddhist ways or whatever other ways—are good if they are taught right and done in a right kind of way, with the right kind of attitude and the right kind of thinking.

To control my thinking, to maintain it, I practice seven days a week. I try to practice it at all times and keep it on a high level. Even when I have a smoke, by my training the first puff of smoke has to be a good thought toward someone, that they feel better, that they get well and be happier. It comes back to me. What you put out comes back to you. Having a lot of good people around me wherever I go also helps me to maintain the power. All of us have to recharge ourselves. I have to take a rest too once in a while. I could be working all the time, but my health would go to pieces.

We have all kinds of helpers at different times. For example, we need helpers when we are doctoring something or healing a person because our minds go kind of blank except for the job to be done. Most old men have some helpers around them who are learning while also assisting and seeing that they protect themselves in the right kind of way. Many of my people have predicted that I'm going to wind up in the hospital myself when I go among the white people or take care of white people. I have to be guided and follow my Indian rules and customs; if I do that completely, I find that I'm protected.

PREPARATION BY PATIENTS

Any traditional Indian knows how to approach a medicine man. There is a certain protocol, a respect for Great Spirit's power. When a person comes to me or any other medicine person, we have questions in our minds and we don't talk too much. It's better if the person coming to us doesn't talk too much.

Whether I want to help someone with a healing is my choice. Healing is not for everyone. It's for people who are sincere, who want to correct themselves, overcome their sickness, their hangups, or whatever else that's been causing their troubles. We do good for good. Before I go into healings the first thing I always want to know is what have they done for my people. If the answer is "nothing," I want to know what they've done for their own people, neighbors, someone down the street. In other words, there must always be a condition brought about where the person himself deserves the healing. There are many people who deserve to be helped and are honestly trying to work with the spirit—Indians, whites, all kinds of people, and race makes no difference when it comes to the spirit.

Our way of life is based on the honest approach, that is, being honest with the Great Spirit, and being honest with oneself. The first step to getting well is to be honest with yourself. Healing begins with the self. I want the patient to take certain first steps in order to want to get well. One of these steps is to clean up his or her thinking. Before people can be cleansed or doctored or whatever you want to call it, they have to get themselves in order with the Great Spirit's power. They have to be ready to give up whatever it is they've been doing that caused the sickness.

In order to get well, you have to give up something. Even Western medical doctors, if they're good, will always advise you to give up something. It might be cake or sugar or sweets or any little thing, but you have to give up something whenever you want to get well. People should realize this. It might be aggression or violence if the patient feels like he doesn't like certain people or wants to make war on someone else. It might be greed. The first thing people have to do if they want to get well is to research themselves and find out what it is that they have done wrong.

I like for people to clean themselves up as best they can before they even come to talk to me. Healing is going to happen if the person is ready. Taking a bath, a sweatbath, may be necessary. I have them take a good bath without perfumes and soap. Some people actually stink with the bad odors of the sickness or the evil spirits that cause it.

When a person approaches me, money should not be involved. I was taught that money should not be involved in healing. It is said among our people that if a medicine man sells his services or commercializes his ability in any way, he'll lose his power. My medicine is always kept noncommercial and on a high level. If there are any demands made, strings attached or conditions, then obviously the healing wouldn't be good. If the patient voluntarily makes a donation, that is acceptable.

A MEDICINE MAN'S PREPARATIONS FOR HEALING

I prepare myself by bathing, maybe a sweat bath, and by right thinking. I won't do a healing if the conditions are not just right, and people have not prepared because of lack of respect or ignorance. I want the place purified too, smoked, so that it has the right atmosphere. The smoke can be incense, cedar, or sage, according to what the original people of that area might have used. If there is a lot of evil present, the area may have to washed clean with a good rain.

I want everything clean and pure so that the healing forces can enter in and feel welcome, and so that the evil spirits will not feel welcome. Women on their moon and babies who might catch the sickness themselves should not be around. Evil spirits can jump from one person to another along with the sickness. If these conditions are not met because someone didn't understand or was disrespectful, bad things can happen and mess everything up. Then all the preparations and the healing would have been for nothing, and a lot of good energy wasted.

It's best to conduct healings in a natural setting in the open air. If too many people started coming to my home to be doctored, it could be bad for my family. I've had trouble of this kind before when I've treated people with mental problems. The problems stayed in the house after the patients were relieved of them. My home is where I live and rest and I don't want negative forces hanging around.

MISUSE OF MEDICINE POWER

I remember a young black fella who was all messed up; he'd been into voodoo and it had turned on him. I think some voodoo practitioners are good, and some of them not so good. Evidently he had learned the wrong way of doing things. He was using it for his own personal power, to enrich himself, rather than to heal people or himself or anything related. He made a lot of money, and he came to me in a Cadillac with Indian jewelry all over him. But he was still going crazy.

I took him to one of my shrines up in the mountains. There's a huge tree with an eagle's nest at its top, and with a spring of healing water that comes from underneath. Over to one side is a rock altar where I make my offerings. After I'm done, the eagle comes down and gets what's left of the offering and carries it off. I only take people to that type of place once. I tell them they'd lose their way if they ever tried to come back. I took this young man there and his mind straightened out fast, at least for a while.

On the way back he told me, "Say, I want you to teach me Indian medicine. If you don't, I'm going to go to those Navajos down in Arizona and they'll teach me."

I said, "No. They won't teach you and I'm not going to teach you either because you'd be dangerous. You'd probably hurt yourself."

Well, he got very angry and cursed at me. In the old days you know, no one would ever question or abuse a medicine person, but times have changed. Anyway, I never said a word.

He went to stay with some Indian people and they took him to doctor some Indian people the same way he had seen me do. What happened was that his hair and eyebrows caught fire. Everyone was scared. This young man was with one of those big bands on the west coast as a drummer, and he had a large following of young people with him. But all of them were frightened too, and they took him to Elko (Nevada) and put him on an airplane for San Francisco. There was a big crowd of people in San Francisco waiting for him to get off the plane, but he didn't get off.

When I went to see people in California they'd ask me where that man was. I'd tell them, "Oh, he'll be coming along. He's all right."

A year and a half went by, and sure enough the young man came in on the same flight he'd been put on over a year ago, but there was no big crowd waiting for him that time. Before he left the airport he called my home and apologized. He said he was all right now and that he had made some changes.

If a person misuses the medicine power, they and anyone around them are going to suffer. To choose good over evil is the key. And if a person has been living right, the right guidance will be provided for you. So it is that medicine men don't want to control anyone, and we won't heal people or use the medicine power to make people do anything against their will. We don't practice that kind of medicine.

The healing way is a circle. I have tried to explain a few things among many to show what is possible in the healing way. *Ho.*

NOTE

1. According to Rolling Thunder, in ancient times when changes in the earth were about to destroy the previous worlds, Indians helped creatures of previous worlds by hiding them in mountains and caves in the inner earth. Some people committed themselves to care for and protect the creatures until the beginning of the Fifth World when they can emerge safely. These ancient beings have great power to help people who are peaceful and at one with Mother Earth.

A teaching by the Seneca people is relevant here. The race of people that live in the inner earth are called Subterraniums. "Our ancestors have carried one hundred thousand years of oral history in their hearts, and we have been told through that history that we came from the inner-Earth at the beginning of each of the four preceding worlds. The Earth changes that ended each world were known by those that listened to the voices of nature. The cavernous tunnels that lead to inner-Earth were opened to some two-leggeds because of their faith and balance. Many of our people still live in the interior world as Guardians of the seeds and Creature-beings that will emerge in the Fifth World." [In Jamie Sams, *Sacred Path Cards: The Discovery of Self Through Native Teachings* (Harper: San Francisco: 1990), pp. 36–37.]

Rolling Thunder, Doug Boyd (author of Rolling Thunder, *published by Dell in 1974), and Mad Bear Anderson (Tuscarora medicine man, one of Rolling Thunder's teachers), in Tucson, Arizona, 1982.*

CHAPTER TWO

Rolling Thunder on speaking tour in Austria, 1980.

The Real History of This Land

"We were here when the earth was young. It shook when we walked on it. That's how ancient we are on this land."

I have had only three past lives so I tell people I'm still a young man. Yet I can talk about things that happened a long time ago because our history has been preserved in writings and teachings for thousands of years.

We Indians come from a different world. Long ago there were greater civilizations on this land than those of the present. Many people think that they learned all about the American Indian in school, but they don't know one thing about us or our history. Many things about the history of this land never appear in history books. In schools all they really have is European history, written at a time when war was being made on us and we were forced to defend the land and our families. This type of history keeps the minds of the people dumb and dull about the things of this land. Examples are when they teach that there was nothing here before Columbus came, that Columbus discovered America, and that certain tribes are extinct. I am talking about real history, not the standard foolishness.

Columbus didn't discover America; everybody knows he was lost. He had a tourist navigator, and the Indians found him and his people and saved their lives. The Indians gave Columbus a lot of good things he and his people had never seen before. The Indians tried to give Columbus some tomatoes, but he thought they were trying to poison him. The Indians took care of these poor lost people who drank only wine, booze, and brandy because the water would spoil—no wonder the Spaniards acted the way they did.

Those Spaniards were deadly little fellows. Columbus put the Indians' hands over a guard rail and whacked them off. Then he captured a few of them and took them back to Spain to exhibit, to prove that he had discovered a new world. The descendants of the ones he kidnapped and took to Spain are still there. Many people from Europe and elsewhere tell me they have Indian blood, and I don't doubt it because a lot of our people were shanghaied on ships to different parts of the world.

The type of people who emigrated to America were oppressed, and some were released from jail provided they would emigrate. Oppression laid a very poor basis for any kind of understanding; they grew fast and by greed took everything. When the pilgrims first landed on this land, the Indians fed them through the first winter. They were taught how to plant corn, which they'd never seen before. The Indians also helped them hunt and shared their provisions with these hungry, homeless people who constantly sought out evil. They thrived on evil. When there were enough of them here, they turned on the Indians, made war on them, and killed Chief Massat's son.[1]

Many so-called extinct tribes do not know that they're extinct. Once when I was visiting San Francisco I met a family of Indians native to that area. According to books by non-Indians, these natives of the area are all extinct, but they're living right there in the middle of San Francisco. This family had the history of that area up to thousands of years ago, to when you could walk on the sand across the bay and fish through the sand in the water underneath. They also had in their possession an article that has to do with holding up the land of that area.

Beginnings

We American Indians have been here a long time. Our history goes further back than even the great flood, of which there is some record in the Judeo-Christian bible. In the Black Rock desert you can see the water marks high on the mountains left by the flood waters. The anthropologists wonder how our ancestors could have put the pictographs in the stone when we didn't have iron or metal. We didn't need metal because the Earth was still warm. The rocks today were mud back then, and our ancestors would carve with their fingers and sticks.

In the beginning there was darkness, and then the Great Spirit caused the earth to be formed. The water and vapor for the earth was still hot. Then came the sun, plant life, fishes, and creatures of the sea. Then the bird life, followed by the animal life, both the two-legged and the four-legged. Animals and man were one and the same at one time.

The races of the world originated in five different places on earth. The people did not come from a single place. The first Indian people came from this land about where North and South Dakota are today. It was swampland, an entirely different climate then, and very hot. There was lots of heat everywhere on the earth at this time of fire by volcanoes everywhere, and the earth would shake when we'd walk on it.

We didn't come yesterday across the Bering Strait and we're not one of the lost tribes of Israel. This was millions of years ago. It is said that we evolved upon this land when the earth was still hot, still moist; and that's what they'll discover one day. We consider ourselves all of one race, but we came from many different places.

Once after a meeting an anthropologist dressed in a business suit walked up to me. He proceeded to tell me where we came from. Before we finished our conversation I explained to him that if I wanted to know where the Jewish people came from I'd go to Jerusalem, find some elderly Jewish people, and ask them. If I wanted to know where the Chinese came from, I certainly wouldn't ask some redneck American. I'd go ask the Chinese and I might get some sense out of it. If I wanted to know where the African people came from, you think I'd ask some paleface in this country? Absolutely not; I wouldn't want an idiotic answer.

I wasn't greatly surprised by his rudeness, but I do admit the blood flowed through me kinda hot for a few minutes. I explained it to him. There were many migrations from everywhere. Before Atlantis went under the sea, the Atlanteans used big boats and could travel in other ways too. They had flying saucers and big canoes and they traveled with the currents when they wanted to. The traditional people who got away before Atlantis went underwater migrated to many places. Some went to Ireland, and they took their knowledge with them. The Cherokee and Irish are cousins. One of our prophecies is that one day the tribe will reunite. So the Cherokee and Irish are naturally attracted to each other and that's why there are so many Irish/Cherokee mixed bloods. Most Indians have O type blood, are allergic to milk, and have no tolerance for alcohol. They're missing an enzyme, and it's the same way with the Irish because the Irish and Cherokee are related.

WE WERE ALL ONE

All original people the world over at one time had a tree of life, when everyone practiced the nature religion based on Mother Earth and Father Sun. The tree of life had its roots in Mother Earth. Drawn in a picture, it showed the branches of the tree like a "Y," and sometimes double branches, but standing straight up. With the coming of the hippies in the 1960s, the tree of life stood upside down, representing the confusion of the modern age people.

According to our teachings, there is room for all under this tree of life. Across the Great Waters in the northern part of Europe, the oak tree was the symbol for the tree of life. The Iroquois in New York state have the maple tree. In the west where we live it would be the piñon tree.

The ancient peoples of all countries and all races at one time knew the ancient ways of how to live together, work together, and sing together. The circle is a symbol shared by all ancient peoples, and that's what it represented. We were all one people at one time, until certain leaders divided people and played one people against the other for reasons such as getting more power, more land, more wealth.

All things are composed of circles, even the atoms in our bodies. That's why we chose the circle in the beginning of time: the circle is the emblem of the Great Spirit. We Native people knew the earth was round at a time when Europeans thought it was flat. The circle on Indian designs has a little break to indicate that we people are not perfect. The circle also means the eye of the Great Spirit looking out.

At one time all people in this land spoke the same language, and this is evident in the drumming and singing. Other people call them chants because they don't understand. All our songs have meaning. Some have words, and some are in the ancient spiritual language that only the medicine people and some of the old ones might understand. It's an ancient spiritual language spoken on this continent a long time ago, before people started dividing up into tribes and speaking different languages.

The Cherokee "war cry" is actually a cry to the Grandfather Great Spirit for help. All people, not only Indians, had their own cry for help from the Grandfather. It can be used at times when people don't have time to make a prayer. When I pass on, you might not hear the Cherokee cry again because not too many people know it nowadays.

For every purpose, there is a different song. We sing a song when we gather the willows so they'll be happy and understand that they're going to be used in a good way. My father told me that long ago when we were at war and the people had to ride a long way, they'd sing to prevent exhaustion and so they'd get there safely.

In the ancient times our people sang when they worked, and when they built the pyramids and the earth mounds. Our songs travel from east to west and from tribe to tribe. The meanings of our songs are taken from the animals, nature, the wind in the trees, water running, and sometimes people, such as in love songs. There are many types of songs, and new ones coming along all the time. Our songs are not something of the past like you might have been taught by anthropologists. Instead, the songs have life and they are here and now. The songs of the land, the original language of the land, are coming back because the land's spirit has returned.

We use the drum and have a high respect for it because

we've seen it work. It brings good energy to us; the drum can remove evil spirits that make us feel tired or bad. The drum is sacred, and when we're drumming and singing you're supposed to be quiet and not go walking around until after the song.

The drum can talk, and I've heard it talk in meetings and ceremonies. I've seen the earth shake underneath the drum and heard a voice come out to give me teachings and instructions. It's told me things that were good for me to know to help guide me. The Great Spirit's beat is the one-two beat like the beat of your heart, and the only kind Mother Earth understands. It's the only kind that relates to Mother Earth on this land, and so the drum is round like Mother Earth, like the universe. The Laplanders, for instance, had the same kind of drum and they danced the same way, in a circle.

When I was in Europe I talked with scholars of that land and spent much time in their libraries. They took me out to see the earth mounds in Denmark and where the Viking kings lived at one time. I heard a Viking song when I was there and it was similar to an Indian song. I could also read the emblems of the Druids and the Vikings. Some friends of mine in Iceland still remember their original Viking ways, teachings, emblems, and designs. They were the same because they had a natural way of life, the same kind of religion that we have here. It was the same at one time around the world. When you go back far enough, there is no difference among the teachings of the ancient spiritual ways of life.

Ancient people could out-think modern man by ten to one. They were of high intelligence and education in the ways of peace, how to build, and how to provide. They had great technology, engineering, astronomy, mathematics—far greater than anything we have today in this society.

Ancient people could accomplish these things because they were clear thinkers and could learn fast; their minds were not cluttered up with trash and greed like today. They could invent whatever they wished; they could create machinery that would never wear out. They could do such things because they had great knowledge used in a good way for the benefit of all. They knew how to use spiritual laws to make things easy.

They had the knowledge of how to move twenty-ton boulders and shape the stones where they couldn't put a knife blade between them. I said "shaped"—they didn't chisel or cut them. They could move huge boulders over vast distances, hundreds of miles, and it was easy. Scientists cannot match these tasks today. They've admitted that even with their modern machinery they can't do it. And thousands of slaves with ropes didn't do it either. This theory is wrong—the ancients couldn't have made a rope strong enough, and they didn't use slave labor. If modern scientists would do a little arithmetic they'd see that the ancients couldn't have fed that many slaves. The slaves would have eaten the entire country out of house and home long before the giant mounds and pyramids could have been built. They had other methods, and it didn't take long to build the mounds and pyramids.

The ancients knew of mathematical formulas and of forces that have not yet been discovered by modern scientists. They even knew how to reverse the law of gravity to make their work easier. The ancient people had energy and transportation unlimited. They could create energy from natural forces, and they knew how to use wind and sun power. They used different types of inexhaustible, nonpolluting energy, such as magnetic fields, the tides, and gravity itself. They could travel anywhere in a very short period of time on this earth and other places.

They had great cities and conveyances without wheels. The ancient people had machines, but they didn't need wheels.

Pollution comes from the mind of a man rather than from machines. When a man invents a machine and he thinks of greed, personal gain, or any other type of wrong thought, the machine is going to pollute; it will be imperfect. The ancient peoples didn't have to worry about that because many of them had pure minds, in accord with all of nature. Everything was in its proper order for a long period of time.

In our ceremonies we put our minds together and use the energy of the sun rising, Grandmother Moon, and the stars. We can put it all together to use these natural forces and those of all good people and the animals of the earth. We can put it all together to heal or move huge stones, whatever is necessary. It's very simple and scientific, and it will eventually become commonplace.

We original peoples of this land had great civilizations and cities. For example, the Incas in South America performed brain surgery ten thousand years ago. They had granaries every twenty miles throughout their lands. Actually, these food stores were not granaries, because they contained different types of food for travelers passing through. People could take out whatever they needed for their llamas and for themselves. The Incas were not concerned about people taking more than they needed.

Cherokee Origins

Some people ask me about where the Cherokee came from. Let's say we came from different directions and different places. Some originated on this land, others from Atlantis, and before that, a seven-pointed star out there. There were seven stars and one of them with seven points. Pleiades, I think you call them, and that's where some of the Cherokee originally came from. The seven-pointed star I wear on my turban represents the star we came from, and is the emblem of the Cherokee nation. The turban too is original Cherokee, and does not come from the movies. It is said that only a real Cherokee can wrap a turban properly.

Machines without wings and wheels brought our ancestors to Atlantis over ten thousand years ago. These people were tall and lighter complected than other Cherokees and other Indians. Some came to the coast of Georgia and the Carolinas, and moved inland to a place called the Smoky Mountains. High in the mountains some of them mixed with the Indians already there. Today there is an entire cove composed of what they call the "white Indians." They are the Assaga,[2] descendants of those who came from Atlantis.

Aminitus Sequoyah was of the Assaga. The Assaga will not talk to you so don't bother to go there unless you speak their dialect. They let me and a few others do the talking; you don't need to bother them or disturb their peace of mind. They are pretty well protected, and they've had a few battles like Indians everywhere.

When I visited the Smoky Mountains I was able to learn about some of my ancestors and their clans. They took me to sacred ceremonial places and I was able to meet with some of the Assaga. It was quite interesting—it's good to know your roots.

THE ATLANTEAN DIASPORA AND OTHER MIGRATIONS

Ancient civilizations like Atlantis declined because leaders abused their power. The leaders were supposed to be spiritual leaders, but they developed egos and jealousy. Even the priesthood became warlike and greedy. Every leader wanted to be a chief, or someone important and powerful. Greed and materialism flourished. There was only one way for them to go then, just like the civilization we are living in right now.

Atlantis was a great island or continent located about where the West Indies are now. In these times only the mountain tops are sticking out of the ocean—Puerto Rico, Cuba, Haiti, the Bahamas. There were great cities with no pollution and no hunger. They used a certain type of crystal as batteries to store energy—a few Indians still know how to use those batteries, which are more efficient and less wasteful than regular batteries. There was commerce by boat into Mexico and with the Mayans. Around the island of Atlantis a great many sea creatures like the one in Loch Ness in Scotland would occasionally wreck the ships and boats.

The people of Atlantis began to forget their original ways and how to get along with nature, and that brought them down. Some of the priests and politicians decided to get rid of the sea creatures, and a great number of people went along with it. They had forgotten the old ceremonies and how to be at peace with the creatures, much like modern people forgetting how to relate to nature. Meanwhile, in some places people retained the original ways and had ceremonies to call the creatures, to feed them, and to sing and talk to them.

The priests and politicians set their scientists and wise ones to creating an explosive based on fission. They set off explosives all around the island and killed most of the sea creatures. Some got away, such as the ones in Loch Ness and Pyramid Lake, Nevada. The creatures went wherever they could go deep enough in water; some of them ended up landlocked, and they still live today.

The explosives also set off great earthquakes, tidal waves, and hurricanes, which caused the land itself to go underwater. The red apples went under with it—that was their karma. Traditionals knew what was going to happen, and so these intelligent people got away. Some went to Egypt and helped build pyramids everywhere they went. Some went to England where Stonehenge is; they placed those boulders perfectly into position to help people know when to plant crops, among many other things about the seasons. Some went south to the Yucatán and other places in Mexico, where the Mayans and Aztecs had great scientists and astronomers; many of their observatories are still standing. The Aztec calendar and clock are far more accurate than the one currently in use throughout the world. Did you know the largest pyramid isn't in Egypt? The biggest one is south of Mexico City, the Aztec Temple to the Sun.

Some of the traditionals went to the Amazon and to Peru, but there was too much fighting there. It took many generations, but the Cherokee headed north again, and brought back with them South American artifacts like blowguns. They came up through Central America and Mexico and rejoined others who had settled in the Smoky Mountains. But everywhere they went, they took their knowledge with them and showed people how to build pyramids and earth mounds.

A great ancestor of mine, Sequoyah, never claimed that he invented the Cherokee alphabet. That's what white people wrote about him. Sequoyah belonged to the Scribe Society, and only the Scribe Society knew about the writings at that time. The original alphabet had ninety-two letters, the same number of letters in the alphabet in Atlantis, where some of the Cherokee originated. Sequoyah revised the written language so that it could be translated into English, and so not be destroyed. At that time white society was making war on my tribe. Now the language has eighty-six letters. At one time, a newspaper was published in our language. Our language is well kept by the Scribe Society.

Not too long ago a great city was discovered underwater near the Bahamas. Divers photographed some of the writing, and it's the same as the Cherokee. They found pyramids sticking out of the mud, paved streets, temples, and metal alloy bars that did not rust and could not be cut with an acetylene torch. In the same area on the shore of a little island was a little village named Cherokee. They don't know how it got its name, of course.

I've never read a book on Atlantis. That's the way it's told in our medicine meetings and the way it's written in our teachings.

Other migrations of original peoples to this land took place later, but long before Columbus. Some were from the east and others from the west. The Vikings who came to Newfoundland were good warriors and honest people, not liars and thieves. The Indians won one good fight with them and then integrated them.

Chinese, Japanese, Mongolian, and other Asians came from the other way to the Indians in the northwest. You might notice that some Indians have slanted eyes. The Chinese came to the Oregon and Washington area outfitted for war. The local Indians were peaceful, so the Chinese went away and couldn't believe there was no war. Some Native peoples did travel across the Bering Strait, and the Eskimos traveled to Lapland. There was communication both ways and still is. In those ancient times, Indians in different places, including British Columbia and Alaska, had huge boats. Doesn't it make sense that some of us went the other way? It wasn't a one-way street; there were exchanges all over the world among ancient peoples.

Nonviolence, the Ancients' Way of Life

We do not believe in aggression, but we do believe that anyone, no matter how peaceful, would defend themselves if necessary. The Shoshone tribe never invaded anybody else's territory, but if someone came among them like the whites did, they acted to protect their land and people. The whites couldn't get a stagecoach through Shoshone territory for seven years. So they had to make a peace treaty in order to get gold from the west to the east coast to continue fighting their civil war.

And then the government put out the word that its politicians wanted to meet with the Shoshone chiefs for the purpose of signing a peace treaty. The word was spread that there would be a big meeting and a feast and that the Indians should come unarmed. Once everyone was gathered, the soldiers brought out an Indian prisoner and shot him dead in front of all the other Shoshoni. That was a warning to them to do as they were told. Then the dead Indian was cut up and cooked in a big pot, also in front of the Indians. It was a gruesome thing: the Shoshoni were forced at gunpoint to be cannibals, to eat their dead brother. The Treaty of Ruby Valley was literally signed in Indian blood.

We don't have any real war dances. Instead, they are called

victory songs or victory dances, and a victory can be over any-thing, such as hunger, sickness, and bad thoughts.

Another example of the misperception about Indians and aggression involves a valley on the old Creek/Cherokee boundary in what is now northern Georgia. Archeologists and anthropologists say a great battle took place between the Creek and Cherokee because they found lots of arrowheads from both tribes. They claim the Indians fought a big war with each other there. But if they had asked me, I could have told them what really happened.

The Cherokee hunted in that valley; it was lush and full of game. One day the Creek came and wanted to claim it as their hunting grounds. Instead of going to war, both tribes decided to play a game of lacrosse. Whoever won would get to hunt in that valley. So they did, and the Creek won the first time. But they had so much fun playing lacrosse, they decided to have another game at the end of the year.

For a long time after that the Cherokee and the Creek would play lacrosse every year. Sometimes the Cherokee won and sometimes the Creek. The valley went back and forth many times. That's why lots of arrowheads are found there from both tribes, not because they fought a big war.

Another favorite in terms of the stereotype about Indians is scalping. Scalping started with the settlers in Pennsylvania and elsewhere in the east when bounties were placed on Indian scalps. Some Indians adopted that practice, as well as whiskey, and then there were many unpleasant incidents.

ON BEING A WARRIOR

According to the traditional ways that the medicine people know, I can tell you that being a warrior does not necessarily mean someone who has killed. A warrior in our ways doesn't necessarily have to be someone crossing the ocean to kill somebody they don't know, dropping a bomb on somebody, or defoliating nature. A warrior is someone who can stand up if necessary and die for his people and his family, or take a bullet in the back in order that others might live. There are many who did. A warrior is a man that believes in the sovereignty of the Great Spirit and stands on his own two feet.

So it was that when a warrior had to go to battle to defend his family or his tribe, it was more honorable to count coup—to strike somebody or dismount him from his horse—than to kill. If a warrior killed someone in battle, he could not enter the camp when he returned. He was placed by his teacher under a tree far to one side. He couldn't even speak to his own family. He stayed there sixteen days until he was cleansed, purified, and got the stink of death off him. So we try not to kill anyone even in battle, if at all possible.

Chief Joseph, one of the great Nez Percé chiefs, looks fierce, and many people see his picture and think he was a fierce man. He wasn't. The United States Army chased him and his entire tribe, including women and children, through parts of Oregon, Idaho, and Montana. He almost made it into Canada. They study his tactics today at West Point to try and understand how he did it. His people's main complaint was that with the soldiers a few miles back, he'd see a flower and he'd have to get off his horse to smell and examine it. If that's what they call fierce or savage, then we need more of them.

We didn't need jails in the old societies. Nor did we need reform schools, orphan homes, or old people's homes. Everyone was wanted, and everyone was cared for. When someone committed a serious crime, and it happened once in a while, they were expelled from the tribe. These people had to live alone and the word was sent out to other Indian camps not to take them in or feed them. There was no other punishment, but that in itself was the worst penalty.

The Shoshoni had a way of taking care of traitors who would scout for the soldiers or otherwise turn traitor to their own people. First, they'd shave the traitor's head. Then they'd shave his ears even with his head and put a ring in his nose. Two warriors would lead him with long buckskin ropes for three days and three nights to a place outside Shoshone country. If he fell, they drug him. And the traitor couldn't look back. He was turned loose and could go where he wanted, but no tribe would want him. Many of them would go up in the hills and live out their lives all alone.

A PAGE IN CHEROKEE HISTORY

My people were driven from their homes in the east to Oklahoma when it was still Indian territory. Some of the Cherokees escaped and stayed on in the mountains. In the European histories, the death march is called the Trail of Tears. We call it the "Bloody Trail" because so many died. The men couldn't defend their women on the Trail of Tears because the soldiers would run a sword through them or bayonet them rather than shoot them, to try to save their bullets. I wrote the following poem about the Bloody Trail.

Cherokee

Where is your heart and which way does your blood flow?
Seems like I heard a soldier saying, Indian, you must go.
You must go westward to a land called Oklahoma.
You can gather your people and go on this Bloody Trail.
You can cry if you want to. It won't do any good.
We're here to steal your land.
We're called the whiteman.
We're here to steal your gold.
You can have your stomp dance and your ceremony too.
But Indian, you're all through.
You must leave the Smoky Mountains and go.
Westward, ho. Let's go westward, ho.
So we built a fire in a kettle, a large kettle.
We kept it going all the way.
We knew we'd be coming back someday.
We knew one thing the whiteman didn't know.
We knew how to pray.
There were many who didn't make it, who died along the way.

Then when oil was discovered in Oklahoma, the oil was stolen, the treaty was broken, and our land was taken from us. There was a big war. Although the history books say nothing about it, the Indians fought them because we don't turn the other cheek. We fought guerrilla warfare, and my father told me how it was. The Indians would raid out to Texas, Louisiana, and into Mexico. They took everything from the Indians so we decided to take a little back. Sometimes we'd take cattle, horses, and occasionally women. Because we were losing so many warriors, the Indians never killed the women and children.

They were captured and taken back to the tribes. That's how my mother met my father.

When I was growing up in Oklahoma, I knew three old people who had been captured by the Indians—two women and a red-haired man who couldn't speak English. He was treated just like any other Indian, and I guess he thought he was an Indian.

The mother of Quanah Parker, one of the great Comanche chiefs, was a white woman, and his father was a Comanche. When the Texas Rangers recaptured her and took her to south Texas, she promptly ran off and returned to the Indians. In just about every case whites captured by Indians chose to stay with the tribes, even after they were offered a choice of whether to stay or return to their homeland, which had to be made after a certain period of time. In some cases they became more Indian than Indians.

Hidden Knowledge and Prophecy

We "savages" developed writing when Europeans were still living in caves. The Cherokee and other tribes have written records of our history from ancient times that were preserved and hidden away. Because they knew the Great Destroyers were coming, the Indians put their writings into sacred caves and then sealed them, such as the one under the Sphinx in Egypt.

Some of us know how the people of Atlantis and other ancient civilizations accomplished great things. You might say, "Well, if it's known, why don't you tell people?" This knowledge will stay hidden until the proper time to bring it into the open. All truly civilized people, including the American Indians, know that too much power and too much knowledge in the hands of fanatics could result in the destruction of Mother Earth. The knowledge would be used for wiping out somebody else or for greedy profit. This type of thinking is demonstrated every day. The writings will stay where they are until such time as modern people get civilized enough that they can live with each other without wars and pollution. The writings and ancient knowledge will not be brought out until such time as people really want to know the truth, and the time is not yet right.

This is a good moment to clear up some other propaganda about the Indians blaming all their troubles on the white man. A long time ago, long before any white men came, we were told by our elders of five temptations. We were warned that if we accepted any of these things that we would lose our heritage and our land. We were told not to accept water that tasted like fire: alcohol. Another was not to accept something for our land that glittered and jingled: money. We were not to put another spiritual way of life in front of ours: Christianity. Next, we were not to put our names to any piece of paper: treaties. And the last was not to intermarry until after the Day of Purification. We did all these things we were warned not to do. My people have suffered a lot, but we don't blame white people for everything that's happened.

Regarding hiding places, my people know a lot about tunnels and caves. When they first started the underground atomic tests near Las Vegas, Nevada, some wells in British Columbia, close to 1,500 miles away, became contaminated. This earth sits on a bubble and opens to the underworld. One opening is located in very rough territory in the Ruby Mountains. There are seven lakes at the top of the Rubies—that sacred number seven again. People really should not try to fish or swim in those lakes, because a lot of people drown. There are many areas and caves sacred to the Indians at the top of those mountains. Most of the caves have residents, and some are guarded by snakes, mountain lions, coyotes, and other kinds of beings. There is also a place where a hole extends through the mountain called Needlepoint Drop, with a cave even to the underworld. It's a well-hidden place, and you couldn't find it by yourself. The only way to find it is with the guidance of a medicine person, and if your purpose is a good one, not simple curiosity. The people living down there can see in the dark, like a horse at nighttime. They went into the cave to get away from the soldiers a long time ago and stayed. There are streams, fish, and heat from ancient volcanoes.

These are not just stories. Because the Indians in this part of the country knew the Great Destroyers were coming, the artifacts and writings were placed in the other world, where they'd be taken care of and not destroyed. The artifacts were placed in sacred caves, which were then sealed. Twenty-seven of these sacred caves are so deep that they go to the fire in the interior, maybe fifty miles or more. Before these caves were sealed, Indians saved themselves from soldiers chasing them by going into the caves, and reemerging on the surface many miles away.

Big Foot, dinosaurs, mastodons, thunderbirds, and other ancient beings relate to this land. According to our prophecies, in the last days these creatures would again walk among us when it is safe. Years ago in the Great Basin they discovered a great silver wolf the size of a small donkey. The Indians knew it was there long before the non-Indian scientists did. Many animals believed to have disappeared a long time ago are returning to the Great Basin, such as the thunderbird. This creature has a wingspan of up to fifty feet, and its name comes from the sound it makes when taking off from the ground.

These animals have been in cool caves, volcanoes, and other places all over this Turtle Island. Indians have been hiding in these places as well. We know the openings to some of these places, but we're not telling at this time because of possible danger. Only Indians can control these huge birds and animals.

A print of one of the Big Foot people, called Sasquatch in Canada and Yeti in Asia, was sent to me years ago by a chief in northern California. There are different races and sizes of the Sasquatch people. For instance, the Yeti in the Himalayas are much smaller than the people in California and British Columbia. The Big Foot people are ancient and some of the first people on this Turtle Island. They are good people, kind and gentle, and not out to harm us.

I heard a story some years ago in California about a young lady who was the only survivor of a plane crash. Because she had a broken leg, the Big Foot people carried her to their camp, and fed her things she could eat, such as roots, nuts, berries. They nursed her back to health and even healed her leg. When she was well three or four months later, they carried her to the highway and left her there so that her own people could find her.

In northern California the army actually searched the mountains and valleys for a Big Foot to shoot and capture so they could stuff him and probably put him in a museum. They didn't succeed. These beings have great powers of making themselves invisible, so that you can't see them at certain times. There were stories about white people who shoot and sic their dogs on them. Then the Big Foot people would get angry and pull the heads off cows or dogs. They are very strong, very powerful; they've picked up fifty-gallon oil drums and smashed them over caterpillar tractors. They are not mean by nature, but wouldn't you be angry if people were shooting at you? These people belong here and should not be shot at or molested by idiots who think they're some kind of super race.

Not too long ago, an old one said that soon we would be building the pyramids again on the ruins of the Great Destroyer civilization. Now that's not a wish, because we don't wish bad luck on anyone. But it is very clear that the present civilization is on its way down.

I'll tell you a bit about the earth mounds. It's said that the builders actually sang those huge mountains of dirt into place just like we sing when we gather the willows. They used songs and magic—or what is generally understood as magic now—to reverse gravity in the same way as was done with the pyramids. That's just skipping over the surface, but that knowledge will be coming back to us just like the songs we sing.

If you study the stars on a clear night, you can see the writing in the Milky Way. Great Spirit's trail is the long tail of the Milky Way, the one we Indians follow. But there is a short trail representing those who came to this land yesterday. In the way it was taught to me, where some of those stars veer into the Great Spirit's trail shows where we are now at this point in time. The stars that veer into the Great Spirit's trail represent other people who are joining us in this land and taking an interest in the ancient teachings. Returning to the ancient way of doing things is good. We can put our minds and hearts together as one and really help toward making things better for all, which is why Great Spirit put us here.

EXTRATERRESTRIALS AND UFOS ARE REAL

Some of the people from outer space are very concerned about the violence on this earth, and they have helped us at times in the past. These people are watching over things so that people on earth will be able to go only so far and no further, because what affects one affects all, and we are in danger of destroying our Mother Earth. They have told me so, and yes, I've met with some of the good ones face to face. There are bad ones out there too, but I've never met with them.

Some years ago I was returning from California and I had an appointment to meet with them in three days. About the time we were pulling through central Nevada, they appeared in the sky in their conveyances and stayed with the train all the way to Carlin. They then landed south of town. I guess it was my white blood that made me so curious about where they landed, but I didn't go to their landing area early. I waited the three days until our appointment, and when I did meet with them as scheduled, they thanked me for being polite and waiting. I think it was a sort of test for me, to see if I'd give in to my curiosity.

They look just like we do, only smaller and usually thinner. They are lighter complected than the average Indian and darker than the average white person. I would say the full-bloods among them, which they mostly are, have an olive complexion. They are highly intelligent and peaceful; they keep their ears covered because their ears are different and kind of pointy. So they wear their hair over their ears or caps over their heads to keep their ears out of sight. There are some of them living among us and taking up our customs and language so that they fit in. They have the ability to speak the language perfectly, wherever they are.

These space beings are watching events on earth and will intervene to prevent people from blowing up the planet, so that what happened once before in our solar system doesn't happen again. Long ago there were twelve worlds in our solar system, including earth, just like there were twelve apostles and twelve poles to a tipi—the number twelve is also a sacred number. Today there are eleven worlds because one of them was blown up by the same kind of crazy barbarian people in the social order like on earth today. They were insane people who couldn't get along with each other and thought they had to blow everything up. These barbarian people thought they had to have war, hunger, and aggression. In their family life and social life they were regressed. They had great technology but were very low on the social order. So they blew up their planet, and that's why the earth doesn't travel in a circle any more. That's why the earth is out of kilter, unbalanced, and why the sun doesn't rise in the east any more.

This earth is suspended very delicately in space. Every atomic blast shakes her up. The scientists and astronomers know these things, but they're pretty quiet, maybe because they don't want to alarm the public. They also know about flying saucers.

We have very close contact. I can't tell you everything about space and space beings, but many of us have had contact with these beings from other worlds. Ancient people did fly around in flying saucers. Big and little UFOs are real, and I've seen them many times.

But why should we be so concerned with what's happening in outer space, when there are so many problems that we need to take care of right here on this earth?

All things are meant to be here, even the insects. All life forms should be preserved and protected. I'm in favor of preservation and protection for Indians too. We need protective laws, not destructive laws. We need special watching over such as stated in our treaties, to see that we don't become extinct too. *Ho.*

NOTES

1. Rolling Thunder was referring to Massasoit, a *sachem* of the Wampanoag tribe at Plymouth, Massachusetts, in 1620 when the Mayflower landed. He signed a treaty of alliance with the colonists in 1621 and attended the first "thanksgiving" celebration. After Massasoit died, his son Metacom (sometimes spelled Metacomet) took his father's place as sachem. Called King Phillip by the colonists, Metacomet was murdered in 1676 by the colonists and his head was exhibited at the fort in Plymouth for twenty-five years. [In *Encyclopedia of North American Indians,* edited by Frederick Hoxie (New York: Houghton Mifflin Co., 1996).]

2. "Assaga" is a phonetic spelling of the name of Atlantean descendants, as articulated by medicine men for hundreds of years.

CHAPTER THREE

Meta Tantay (Nevada), circa 1982.

Things to Come

"All prophecy is subject to change."

O ut on the reservations we older ones often sit up all night talking about the prophecies and putting them together so that by morning we have a more accurate picture than you would have by reading newspapers or watching television. The Indians are here to help and guide wherever we're invited and wanted. You hear the same prophecies from tribe to tribe—to the east with the Iroquois, the north to Canada, and in South America. The prophecies go on and on; our teachings are quite extensive.

It is said that when the plants and animals cannot live, then man cannot live either. This is not a very encouraging picture, but don't panic. The most helpless people will be those who don't know what's coming. It might be sooner than you think. But I'm not here to talk about doomsday—I'm here to wake you up.

I remember when there was a lot of talk about California going underwater. In those days foreign gurus had set a date, and they didn't ask us. We knew that San Francisco was not going underwater, because the time had not yet come. According to prophecy, a time will come when California goes underwater. The only people who know the law of this land are certain Indians. You have to know which Indians to ask; many of our people have wandered away and some have assimilated, and they do not have this knowledge. The Indian's job is to know the law of the land, and how to take care of the land and nature. When we walk, we know the meaning of every plant, rock, or anything that moves in the forest. Other people are supposed to do other jobs, but the law of this land is the Indians'. Wherever traditional Indians are living, there is nothing to fear because we'll hold up this land.

According to our teachings, there's no way anybody else is going to live on Turtle Island if we Indians become extinct, and by that I mean live as free people, unoppressed, with plenty for all. In other words, people should follow whatever lifestyle fits them, as long as it isn't oppressive to anyone else and is in harmony with Great Spirit's ways.

Disasters can be prevented by ceremonies that fit this land and show thanks to the Great Spirit in proper ways. The authority to care for this land was given to us long ago before anyone else came to this land. It's our job, and nobody else is going to do it. Of course, we need the cooperation and good intentions of other people in order to clean up the pollution and destruction.

We do what we have to in peaceful ways to protect sacred lands and burial grounds. Certain shrines and springs, among other things in this country, are being protected by the Great Spirit. We're taking them back in our own way of doing things through the Great Spirit. Many years ago the Tennessee Valley Authority wanted to build a dam that would have flooded our sacred lands and burial grounds. Some medicine men conjured up that little darter creature that scientists said was extinct. When the darters were discovered, different groups began fighting among themselves about whether to build that dam.

I have doctored hot springs to prevent "civilized" people from using them for electric power plants, greenhouses, and a half dozen other things. For example, some years ago about six different parties were fighting over the hot spring north of our camp. As long as they fought and competed among themselves, they didn't have time to fight with us. If they ever got together, we'd never have been able to use the spring; it would have been lost to us.

The weather itself has changed. The rains used to come in seven-year cycles, but now the weather has gone crazy. The weather can be predicted in this area now only one day at a time, although we Indians can do somewhat better than that. Storms are always good. Mother Earth is out of balance and needs a cleansing. Indian people here used to have ceremonies to give thanks for keeping things in their proper balance. No one else is going to do that; it's our job.

Until the Sixties I didn't know of any white people who were really interested in Indians or in wanting to share with us as brothers. If they had listened to us thirty or forty years before then our natural resources could have been preserved, but back then if a white person talked to us it was to tell us to go to hell. Anyway, in the Sixties things started to evolve and change. I saw young people wearing long hair, beads, sandals, which were more in accord with ancient traditions than the way people usually dressed. The young people started to come to us, as the Hopi prophecy said. Now there are many, young and old, who are friendly toward us and interested in learning the ways of this land.

The time has come again for Indians to travel, communicate without intimidation, and seek out our brothers among all races. In the late 1960s a group of medicine people from all over the world had a meeting in Oklahoma, the first one in over one hundred years. At this meeting, an ancient board was brought out with writing on it that said the spirit of brotherhood will be born again among the Native peoples here in this land and then will spread all around the world.

About fifty of us Indians went across the Great Waters to attend the World Ecology Conference. There were people from Africa, Asia, and all the European countries. We found that many different nationality groups were not speaking to each other. The Vietnam war was underway and they were getting ready for the next war. The Swedes weren't talking to the Americans because they thought the Americans were all CIA agents. The Dutch and the French were not talking to the Germans because some of them remembered the concentration camps. When the Laplanders joined us we had a sunrise ceremony together, and that night huge numbers of people danced in a circle like the ancient peoples used to dance long ago. We taught them how to dance in the circle all over again. By the next morning you couldn't tell who belonged in which camp, where before almost everyone stayed in their own camps.

Purification

If we don't heal this planet, Great Spirit—the one known as God, Jehovah, Allah, the same one who put all of us here—is going to take over and clean it up. Unless people learn to observe ancient teachings, honor Mother Earth, live harmoniously, and learn how to pray again, there will be great upheavals.

These upheavals are a result of the abuse of Mother Earth and the breaking of treaties. The Great Dustbowl in Oklahoma was brought about by the breaking of the Treaty of Neosho. That treaty said that as long as the water runs and the grass grows, Indian territory would not be incorporated into a state. By their own words and the breaking of their word (Oklahoma was granted statehood in 1907), the white man predicted his own punishment.

Our prophecies predict a period of forty years of pollution of the land, air, and water that is so severe only a few will survive. We call this the Day of Purification, and for many white people, it is the Day of Judgment. It's the same thing and the cycle has already started—four decades of destruction, natural disasters, and a general breakdown in society. Only a few places will be safe, and it will be the end of modern society as we know it.

Mother Earth has been mistreated. The earth is a living body just like we are. It is said among our people that the earth sits on a bubble, like oil with water under it, that holds it up. Mother Earth floats, slips, and slides on a core of molten rock, and is subject to earthquakes and other natural phenomena. These bubbles are also waters, lakes, streams within the earth that nourish and feed people and all other beings. These waters are networked throughout the earth.

Mother Earth has a way of cleansing herself when she's been violated too much. She turns over just like an animal turns over in the sand to cleanse itself of parasites. There are too many parasites on the earth, and they take and take and never give. No offerings are made when trees are cut. There should be a law such as in Denmark and Sweden that obligates everyone who cuts a tree to plant one. White men got this land for nothing but the taking, so they don't respect the land. The earth will turn over like it did eons ago. The proof of her turning over is in Alaska, where there are mastodons and dinosaurs with tropical food in their mouths perfectly preserved in ice.

Every time an atomic blast goes off, the earth shakes a little and the North Pole shifts. Magnetic north is not the same as it used to be. If the earth turns over, it will cause changes in the weather, and we might be where the North Pole is or down in the Antarctic. It is said that the sun will reverse its course, rising in the west and setting in the east.

Pollution is an illness spreading through the body of the earth. Some people claim they don't know how to clean it up. But I've seen a huge cement plant in Denmark with nothing being released into the air. The Danes told me they spent six million dollars cleaning up the plant. I saw another plant in Fernley, Nevada, spewing dust over the whole town. People finally got together and sued the plant owners for damages, so the plant was cleaned up to a certain extent. But there's still a lot of material coming out of smokestacks. They could have done a better job; and they have the technology. Do not let them try to persuade you that they do not have the technology. The fact is, they could spend some money on this type of technology instead of going to the moon or making more atomic bombs and other weapons.

In Alaska I visited the coast, where I saw the second highest tide in the world. You could almost see the water rising and falling. I got to thinking about why someone doesn't put a platform out there with gears and a turbine to use that energy. They'd have all the energy, electricity, they wanted. One person shook his head and said, "Maybe the oil companies wouldn't like it." I don't understand these "civilized" ways where greed and money are gods.

Civilized man talks of harnessing nature, conquering nature, and making nature a servant to man. This shows that civilized man doesn't know the first thing about nature and nature's ways. Nature is sovereign and must be respected. All life and every single living thing is to be respected. That's the only answer. You can't control nature, and you can't fight with nature and win. There's more energy in one bolt of lightning than the first atomic bomb dropped on Japan.

There is an order to all things in nature. The land gives food, shelter, medicine, and cleansing. The land belongs to life and life belongs to the land. The Great Spirit is the life in all things—all creatures and plants and even rocks and minerals. Too many people don't know that when they harm the earth they harm themselves. Nor do they realize that when they harm themselves, they harm the earth.

Signs and Timing of Prophecies

All prophecy is subject to change. The Great Spirit is the one who decides when things should be changed or the earth cleansed. Nobody else can do that, including medicine men. Anybody who tries to decide these things or claims to know exactly when things will happen is making a mistake. Don't expect us to set a date like those foreign gurus do.

The time is coming, and whatever your karma is, you won't get away from it. We do not contradict the scientists; scientists are getting closer and closer to being accurate according to what ancient people have known for ten thousand years. The last days are very close now. But the thing that amazes me is that while they know these things, they provide no solutions about what to do. Scientists seem to think they can't do anything. If spiritual people get together and put things back in their proper order, the prophecies can be changed. Anyone can be a spiritual person, and you don't have to be an Indian.

Don't be like that old man sitting there on a volcano in Oregon. He said he wouldn't move, and it blew up on him. Now he's under thirty feet of ash. Don't be like the dumb cows that stand on the railroad tracks watching the train coming at them. When are people going to wake up to facts? When an Indian tells you something you can just figure it's true. We don't know everything, but when it pertains to this land, are you going to look east or west to some foreigners?

The Great Spirit tries to give people warnings to return to the proper order. In the 1960s two stars changed places as a sign that the world needed to be warned to change its ways. The earth itself is giving us warning signals. We'll have many signs to inform us about what we must avoid, and it's good to know those signs.

You can judge by the signs around you. All you have to do is look into the clouds. They talk to me. You can see faces in those clouds—animals, people, different things. The clouds will learn to talk to you. You could even learn to understand the thunder—it has a powerful voice and always delivers a message. You could look into the stars in the sky until you learn how to read them. Some of the stars represent great warriors who have passed on, and they show the way.

It is also said that in the last days prehistoric era beings will return, such as dinosaurs, thunderbirds, and the great silver wolf. In some areas, the great silver wolf and thunderbirds have been seen. Two wolf pups were recently shot and killed in California, one weighing 180 pounds and the other 245 pounds. These animals were just pups, not even fully grown. The great silver wolves are coming back, and it is said that the trails will not be safe except for Indians and others who know how to relate to these beings. But the return of these beings is a good sign. All beings are needed and placed here among us for a purpose—even the ants belong here.

The birth of the white buffalo calf was a signal to us to withdraw from the white man's violence and greedy ways, and to return to our original spiritual ways. Other white buffalo calves are supposed to be born in different places and to different tribes. One is supposed to be born in this area, and that one is a sign to the local Indians to retreat into the mountains and caves for protection against the fighting armies.

The ancient prophecies predict that just before the next world war breaks out, one-third of the sky will light up blood red when the full moon rises. The red will represent the blood to be spilled.

Ten new diseases with no modern cures will spread. AIDS is one of them. There are natural cures for these diseases, but conventional doctors and scientists will not know them. Indians have cures for everything.

I've seen lakes in northern Sweden that are dead because of acid rain. The acid rain came from England and other western European countries. I've heard a great deal as well about the acid rain in New England where the trees are dying. In most places I see lots of pollution and the trees dying from the top and falling over. When they almost touch the ground, that's when the land is ready to go. In some places like New York and Los Angeles, the people are not really living. It's as if all the concrete in the cities has turned the people to concrete themselves.

I've had visions of the purification, and it's truly a horrible thing. The earth itself, the air, and the water will all be polluted. As with the cleansings of the past, which were by a great flood and before that by fire, the next time will be by both fire and water. It is said that volcanoes will open up again. We can point to the ones that will go first. There will be seventeen volcanoes erupting up and down the west coast, and there are fifteen to go now. The earth itself is heating up. In places such as eastern Montana volcanoes are starting to appear where they have never before existed.

When I visited people in Salt Lake City, they took me up on a mountain where Brigham Young first brought people into Salt Lake City. You could see the whole city from that mountain. They asked me what I thought. I said, "I don't think, I *see* it as it was, as it is, and as it's going to be. That broad avenue right down below us, I see fire coming out from under the streets and the sidewalks, and that's where your city will split apart."

And they said, "That's odd. Your statement is the same as in our Book of Mormon. Also that's where the earthquake fault is." Now nobody told me about the earthquake fault and the Book of Mormon. All I saw was a smooth, broad street, but I have a different way of "seeing."

I've heard about the hole in the ozone layer caused by chemicals and how the harmful rays are getting through. The earth is warming up and melting the ice because the ozone and air are getting thinner. That big hole is hundreds of miles across and growing. Some Indians from Yakutat, Alaska, came to visit me because the glacier near their village was coming closer.

First, they called in some Catholic priests to stop the glacier, but the good fathers couldn't stop it. Then they called me and I told them what to do. I recommended that they return to their Indian ceremonies to stop the glacier. The elders went out and did what I told them and they slowed it down, but the movement needs to be slowed down still more. Yakutat is a beautiful fishing village, but it's only temporary. I know that a time will come when they will have to evacuate that little village.

We are now moving into the last stages where the weather is disturbed, with all kinds of storms, cyclones, tornadoes, and earthquakes breaking out. There will be up to thirty feet of snow in the great cities of the northeast, snow where it's never snowed before, earthquakes on the west coast, floods one year and droughts the next. Confusion will multiply.

I know of places far north where they grew corn. The corn doesn't grow anymore because the weather is upset. The growing season is getting shorter and the winters heavier. Ash from Mount Saint Helens went all the way across the country to Florida, like we knew it was going to do. It killed the honeybees and moths that pollinate the crops.

According to the prophecies of the last days of the purification, people will be freezing, starving, and homeless. Everything will come to a stop—there will be no trains, no cars, no airplanes moving.

Before anyone from Europe came to this land it was written on the rocks that a great gourd of ashes will drop on this world and pollute it. War comes from cultural pollution, from the human brain, evil minds. But this will be the last war, and there will be no winners. The big cities will be the first to go. There will be much destruction and a great many people destroyed.

We Indians have been told that atomic fallout is now

beginning to mutate plants, animals, and humans. It is said that in the last days we will not be able to tell whether the babies born are boys or girls, and that children would be born with hair on their heads and teeth in their mouths and be far in advance of their years. The plants have started to mutate; we've been instructed to put away a two-year supply of food and good seed, not hybrids. The old plants will fail and not produce true.

There will be no money for police and armies. Confusion will multiply, with more crime and delinquency. Like any sickness it will spread, and it is spreading everywhere now like a cancer. The worst delinquency of all is right in the world's financial capitals, such as New York City.

There will be famine because crops won't grow. It's really surprising how many differences among people cease to exist when a person gets really hungry day after day and month after month. If you've never been there or don't remember the last Great Depression, I can tell you that the coming famine will be worse.

The famine will start in the cities. With no food in the stores, people won't know what to do. Most of the survivors will turn on each other because that's all they know how to do, just take. They don't know what to do with their hands or how to grow anything anymore. Because of heavy snows in the midwest and northeast, snow in Florida, volcanoes in the northwest, and floods, earthquakes, and smog in California, refugees and other people will head for Arizona.

I have seen in a vision that survivors will come walking out of the cities. Thousands of hungry and cold people will leave California, walking down I-80 carrying their belongings on their backs. They'll spread out to the countryside and some will try to buy their way into safe places, but their money will have no value. It is said that a time will come when a good blanket will be worth more than gold and many people will be turned away.

ROLLING THUNDER'S VISION

I looked into these things a long time ago. I had to know what was going on so I'd know how to cope, or if there was a chance for corrections to change the course of events. I've seen the day when San Francisco and many other great cities will be broken rubble, only concrete left. I saw the earthquakes, the fires breaking out, the volcanoes. I have seen soldiers fighting among the rubble of buildings.

It appeared as if there had been a big war and concrete was strewn everywhere. The armies were fighting but it seemed like I could walk anywhere; they couldn't see me. In the vision I thought that they weren't bothering Indians anymore because they had their own problems. Then Spirit told me they'd already taken everything—they'd already stolen everything and they didn't need nor want anything from us anymore.

Then the soldiers faded away and there were no more armies or police because there was no money worth anything to pay them. But there were armed bands roaming around. Survivors came crawling out of basements, and turned on each other and started beating each other's brains out. There were no bullets left, but they were still fighting each other for any scrap of food, and soon there was no more food. They didn't know what to do; store shelves were empty. Gangs started roaming the countryside looking for food. They didn't know how to grow food, but only take. There were no cars, no transportation, no gas to be had. People everywhere were jobless, hungry, desperate, and cold.

A different kind of army came into being. This army was led by an American Indian. He wore a cap with a red seven-pointed star on it. There were officers, in perfect formation and well fed. The strange thing about this army is that they were all on horseback and had no guns. They went into the great cities on horseback, rescuing what they could, bringing food and medicine to the starving people. The leader always asked when he came upon a group of people, "What have you done for my people?"

The army led by the Indian in the red cap took many babies. They seemed to know that if the babies were raised in the Indian way that they would grow up all right as warriors for peace. Many of the old ones were left to die.

On Changing Prophecy

All prophecy can be changed. These things are what may happen under present conditions, but conditions don't have to stay the way they are.

Native Americans offer a solution to the world's problems. People are interested in this message because they know the end is approaching, and they have to do something different to survive. Many people are depressed and stressed, but that only draws more negativity to them. We offer people hope for a peaceful world by sharing our message with them.

People have to conquer their egos and realize that we are one with all living things, that we are no better than the rocks, trees, and animals. We must realize that everything on earth is here to be preserved, not abused and destroyed. The white man has wasted his labor and resources, and our prophecies say that will not continue for much longer. The healing should begin here in this land, because here is where the abuse, the greed, is the worst.

People must change so that they think with their hearts and minds. We must learn to walk softly upon Mother Earth. If enough people prefer peace, there will be peace. If spiritual people get together and put things back in their proper order, the prophecies can be changed. It would take a lot of people who believe in truth, peace, and justice.

I understood a long time ago that when the right time comes, some people will be there to help put things back in their proper place. People of all races will join together to fight for peace. It doesn't matter what color you are, but rather where your heart is and which way your blood flows. We recognize that there is room for all people to be here or they wouldn't be here.

It was predicted that someday we would find our way back to our homeland, and return to our Native ways. Part of the prophecy is that we Indians will take over, which includes people who are Indian in their hearts. Millions of us will return to our homeland. At one time our population was reduced to one-half of one percent of the entire population. But we are coming back, and some will be reincarnated Indians.

A few years ago, parents of a young white lady came to me. They were concerned about their daughter because she liked everything Indian. She dressed like the Indians, wanted to be around Indians, and wouldn't have anything to do with her parents' white friends. So I had a smoke and looked into it. I saw that in a previous life this young lady had been an Indian, and her camp was raided by the white soldiers. All the men, the warriors, were gone from the camp. The only people there were women, babies, and old ones, but the soldiers opened fire on the people in the camp, killing everybody. The women screamed and cried out and held up their skirts to show the soldiers that they were women, but the soldiers killed them anyway. This young white woman was there, and she had a baby. The soldiers killed her baby in front of her before they killed her, and so she died hating the white man. In her next life she came back as a white person so that she could get over this hatred. When I told her rich white parents this, they asked me to doctor her, to change it with her so that she would be happy by not following the Indian way. But I wouldn't do it.

People who are willing to hear and practice the truth can assist their fellow man by helping to turn the prophecies around. And they will not need guns. Guns and such should be a thing of the past. For lack of another name, I call people who want to hear the truth the Thunder People.

If there are enough Thunder People, modern civilization doesn't have to go down. I have worked with many people in this country and in Europe, as well as with the Eskimos in Alaska, to help them return to the old ways. It would be much better if many people survive, so that's what we're working on right now. I believe that the more people who change their thinking and become Thunder People, the better everyone's chances of survival. There is no guarantee in this life for any individual, nor for any nation or government.

SURVIVAL

World War III will be followed by forty years of purification. We may go through hard times, but even so we can make it easier on ourselves; we can survive.

A lot of people come to the desert and say they want to learn how to survive. They think they're going to learn a few plants for medicine and food, and maybe how to meditate, and that they're going to survive. That's okay for themselves, but they're not thinking about their neighbors. If you can have gardens and grow food, you ought to be practicing.

Love the earth. Treat it gently and it will reward you. To choose a simple life close to nature during the purification period is the beginning of survival. Walking softly on the Mother Earth means living in tune with nature and living as self-sufficiently as possible. The main things I think people should learn are to take care of their health and to store food in any way they can. People must learn about wild plants and how to use their hands again to produce their own food. Survival will, however, require more than learning about a few plants and medicines: people must return to a life of the spirit.

We look to the future and prepare for it. All of us have a lot of work and learning to do before it gets rough, and we should be preparing for survival. We need more people trained in how to grow things, and to replant the piñon nut trees.[1] We need to train people how to grow food crops in desert alkali and salt. At our camp, Meta Tantay, we were trying to be self-sufficient.

Meta Tantay

I hadn't planned to start a camp in the desert, but when my sons were boys they wanted this land. There was nothing on it. The old white fella who owned the land seventy years ago gave it up and said nothing would grow because there was too much alkali in the soil and no water. But I thought that buying the land would help my sons settle down and learn more about nature. When I went out to look at the land, a golden eagle flew overhead, circled around, and flew off to the east, so I knew it was a good place and meant to be. I'd sat with the old ones and I knew the history of that land.

Our camp was located in a position exactly like where they built earth mounds and pyramids, that is, in the middle of four sacred mountains. There is a mountain for each direction and the highest one to the north is shaped like a pyramid. The camp was a high-energy place where the lightning strikes most often. It is said that our camp was a place of power where people get well.

We lived together with nature and worked with nature rather than struggling against it. We found water in a well at seven feet and another at twelve feet. I believe in scientific methods and technology, so I used a willow stick. When that stick broke, that's where I drove the stake in the ground. Anyone can develop the ability to witch for water.

I made offerings to the water in the creek nearby, because it has a life too. If we don't show the proper respect, then the water is liable to go away. There was an old rusty pipe sticking out of the ground, the only thing left from the old white man's dry well. It reminded us to make offerings and prayers of thanks before taking anything from the land. We made offerings before butchering our livestock and before picking anything from the gardens. And there was no waste—everything was put to good use.

We lived in wickiups that we built ourselves with willows without government help and bank loans. When we gathered the willows, we made offerings and took only what we needed. The willows were woven like an upside-down basket. You dig down into the ground a little way and that makes them cool in the summer and warm in the winter. We covered them with canvas, old rugs, and some recycled nylon material. We also used recycled fence materials. Some years ago in Marion County a man named Cristo built a fence across the county, and we just happened to have a truck down there to load it up when they tore it down. We built wickiups that were strong and earthquake proof. Once some people in Elko (Nevada) were harassing us about building codes. I told them that our tipis and wickiups would be standing when their buildings fall to the ground.

We planned to make our own gas, because the prophecies foretell energy shortages that will halt all oil-powered transportation. We kept horses and were told to keep our legs strong for the same reason. If you want a horse to pack through the mountains, a wild horse after he's broken is more sure-footed than a tame horse. He won't fall over a cliff where a tame horse will. If you want a horse for herding cattle, why then a mustang is best. If you want a horse for racing, one that doesn't have the brains to turn when he should, then you gotta have a thoroughbred.

We used wind power, including a big windmill over a well to pump water to irrigate our gardens. And we were looking into using wind to power our generators. I liked the electric propane motors too because they are more efficient (burn cleaner) and last longer. It's very easy to convert the propane motors to methane, and you could easily make your own methane.

We used solar power to heat water for showers and washing dishes. After three hours of sunshine, the water was 130 degrees Fahrenheit. It was too hot to take a shower without getting scalded, so we had to add a cold water system to mix with the hot.

We built a huge machine shop to work on old cars and trucks. Mechanics worked there all the time, and they were fast. When they'd overhaul a motor it ran better than when it was new. We used old farm machinery that you just pull behind the tractor, not fancy hydraulics and expensive stuff. The older machinery breaks down less. We'd take parts off the cars that people sometimes left at the camp, strip them down, and use the iron and parts. Nothing was wasted.

When we hunted, we didn't stomp over the land and waste things. We'd hunt in a spiritual way. We would go through certain ceremonies to be clean when we went hunting, such as smoking ourselves. If I got tired of hunting, I'd sing my medicine or deer song and make a clean kill right through the heart or the neck—the deer has to drop right there. Then we drink the blood of the first deer, maybe eat some of the liver, and make an offering. We have to make an offering to every animal we take, as well as an apology for the life of that animal. There was no such thing as sport hunting, that is, hanging a rack on the wall or showing what a big hunter somebody is.

Feeding our families is a serious business, and every part of an animal has to be used. We would use every part of the animal, and thereby show our respect and gratitude. We'd gather herbs, and even the bees would move back because they knew we were taking only so much and would leave some for them. People communicate with insects, animals, and birds, whether they know it or not. People who are in harmony with nature issue a certain energy and the animals understand.

This land that they said we would starve to death on was very good to us. The desert was like a jungle, green in every direction. We had four big gardens at one time, with cabbages two feet across and turnips so big they wouldn't fit in a gallon bucket. Remember Findhorn in Scotland? I've met some of the people who live there, and they are fine people. I think we were doing just about the same thing they were, that is, growing things in a harsh climate with a short growing season. There are only forty to forty-five days in a growing season in north-eastern Nevada.

We put some of the gardens in beds made with railroad ties. Rocks were put under the ties and we fertilized the beds real well with natural fertilizer. We didn't use chemical fertilizers because they burn and kill the soil. Instead, we used manure from the livestock and humus material from our compost pits. When we irrigated the beds, the alkali and salt washed out of the soil.

Traditionally, the desert provided the tribal people who lived here with all the food they needed to survive. Plants that were tough enough to grow here naturally were strong with the spirit of the land, and that made them good medicine as well as good food. Many of the wild foods no longer grow here.

At one time juniper trees covered these mountains. Along the streams were cottonwood, willows, and aspen. But when the first white people came to this country they cut them all down for hundreds of miles around. The trees were used to feed the big ore smelters and make cross ties for the railroad. They couldn't grow back because they also brought their sheep, cattle, and horses with them and overgrazed it. Juniper and piñon trees were knocked down over thousands of acres so that a few more blades of grass would grow for cattle. The grass lasts only a couple of years and then nothing grows because there is nothing to hold the soil in place.

We collected seed from the hardiest and healthiest plants so that each generation we grew was stronger and made us stronger. Grandmother Moon plays an important part in growing plants. We planted according to the phases of the moon, which is ancient knowledge used by original peoples.

We had bugs but we controlled them without poisonous, polluting chemicals. Nonchemical bug control is easier and you don't have to spend a lot of money for poisonous insecticides, such as that med fly business years ago when they sprayed everything and everyone. It seemed rather like using a sledge hammer to kill a mosquito or an atomic bomb to kill a small animal.

Once when grasshoppers and other bugs were eating lots of big holes in our cabbages, I was getting ready to go on tour and didn't have time to think about making up natural sprays. So I had a smoke and thought about it and then went out and had a talk with the birds. The birds came in by the thousands and cleaned out those bugs. Nowadays in Carlin in the summer they do aerial spraying to kill mosquitoes, but the spraying also kills hummingbirds and nighthawks, both of which eat many times their weight in mosquitoes.

We didn't kill anything unnecessarily. Only mice and rats were freely exterminated if they came into our homes, because they carry diseases and get into the food in the kitchen. All they're good for in the first place is to feed the coyotes and wild animals. I think mice and rats are kind of like some politicians: they have no respect for people and no boundaries.

We don't kill other wildlife, including spiders, scorpions, and snakes. The band of coyotes to the north of the camp never bothered any of our livestock. I made an agreement with them—that's part of a medicine man's job. The coyotes would go five miles away to the white ranchers' stock instead. We didn't hunt or trap the coyotes, but rather we prayed for them.

We had an agreement with each other and respected each other's territory.

The people who lived in the camp also treated each other with respect. When I said we recycled everything, I meant it— we even recycled people and restored them. Meta Tantay in the Chumash language means "go in peace." And that's what I tried to teach the people in the camp: to be at peace with themselves, each other, and nature; to have self respect; and to stand on their own two feet. People were taught not to be helpless, but instead strong and self-sufficient in the way that the Grandfather Great Spirit wants us to be.

Thus, we put the ancient teachings together with certain modern ways and the results were good. Not everything invented by modern civilization is bad: it depends on where the invention comes from and how it is used. We proved at Meta Tantay, although we weren't trying to prove anything, that it is possible to live in the modern world in harmony with nature.

We Indians are getting ready for survival because we will suffer as well, and we don't want to be in the same canoe with or party to the wrongdoings being committed. That's the reason for camps such as Meta Tantay, where we study and teach people who want to learn how to survive.

After the Purification

According to the prophecies, if the white man does not maintain the treaties we will take all the land back. But what are we going to do with it? We'll need all the help we can get for the next hundred years to clean it up. So we need the white people and they need us.

The future will bring great things. Survivors—mainly

people experienced in a spiritual way of life and living in tune with nature—will move into an area where the earth has been purified. In this area, there will be no more wars and no hunger. There will be a way of knowing who has a good heart, and who is honest and who is not. Those who have a good heart will join together and share in a way never before possible, get along with each other, and accomplish great things.

Great civilizations will rise. A time will come when ancient technologies will be available once again, and we will be able to invent anything we want without pollution, without fouling up the water, the air, and the earth itself. The ancient peoples knew the magic, the songs, and the formulas that worked with one another.

I see a Thunder People rising
Like those of long ago.
Great cities are appearing,
I see that it is so.
Cities clean, air is pure
Clean water's drink is mine.
I see from the farthest mountain's view
No violence and no crime.
But first the cleansing storm must come,
Mother Earth will have her way.
First we'll start with some volcanoes
Sixteen more to blow.
Then throw in a drought or two
And thirty feet of snow.
Then I see a Thunder People rising
Many I have seen before.
The injustice and destruction

No longer to ignore.
I want to see a hundred miles
Whichever way I look.
Starting with a million people
Who knew just what it took.
                    —ROLLING THUNDER
                       Chief of the Thunder People

Eventually there will be new tribes and new families springing up. There will be a new society without the "isms" and know-it-all factions. It'll be beautiful. *Ho.*

NOTE

1. In this instance and elsewhere, Rolling Thunder is referring to the destruction of Nevada's forest lands by the Bureau of Land Management. Thousands of acres of piñon nut trees were "chained" down on Indian treaty territory. The Bureau used bulldozers dragging an anchor chain, which ripped the trees out of the ground. Because piñon nuts were a major source of protein for the Indians of the region, their destruction threatened the Indians' traditions and welfare.

Sign posted at entrance to Meta Tantay, circa 1979.

Rolling Thunder standing in front of the Thunder Trading Company & Frontier Deli, 1979. He was part owner of the business, which specialized in serving healthy (not health) foods.

CHAPTER FOUR

Rolling Thunder and Spotted Fawn, 1980.

The Clan Mothers

"We are taught that our women are sacred."

Although there are Indian women more qualified than I am to talk about women in our societies, I will talk a bit about them. I don't think anything in the medicine way can be complete without recognizing women. We do allow the women in some of our ceremonies. It wouldn't be fair to them not to allow them in, but they have their own ceremonies too.

The clan mother is the one with the most authority in any Indian camp. I know that many people think the chiefs and medicine men are the ones who run everything, but don't you believe it. The clan mother is a very powerful person, and when the clan mother speaks, I listen. The clan mothers' power may be behind the scenes, but it's there all the time, and only a woman can break a chief or medicine man. A clan mother can dehorn a chief or medicine man so that he can never practice again. No one else can do that, and I've seen it done once.

When I was among the Iroquois in New York, I saw a very powerful young man who was both a chief and a medicine man, which is very rare. He had many followers, but he'd been overruling the elders, misusing his powers, and forming cliques that caused dissent in the tribe. We were in the longhouse when it happened. When he moved to stand up to speak, he never made it to his feet. Before he could stand, the clan mother stood up, pointed her finger at him, and said, "Sit down! We do not want to hear what that man has to say. Be seated."

And the young man sat down. If he hadn't or if he had been that rude, there were members of the Warrior Society standing on either side of him, and they could have grabbed him in a minute. He knew that. Now he can never be a chief or medicine man again as long as he lives. He never said a word—he was fired, dehorned. He got old and ugly fast after that. He could come home only once a year to participate in the ceremony for the dead, but he can't stay after sundown. That's how strict we are, the way of our discipline. And that's also one of the reasons many of our women do not see the need for "liberation."

I like to raise strong men and women; we need to be strong. The Grandfather Great Spirit likes people to be clean and strong in their thinking as well as their bodies. My young people are warriors, including the girls. There were warrior women too in the old days—not Sacajawea or Pocahontas or traitors like that. Some of our women fought the fiercest when the soldiers went to the camp when the men were gone. Some of them were the best of all warriors, especially when they had to protect their young. There are names of women warriors not recorded in your histories, but they are still remembered in our histories.

There have been many great women highly respected among our people to this day for their positions in life. The chief of the Cherokees in Oklahoma only a few years ago was a great lady named Wilma ManKiller. I've heard many good things about this woman. The Hopis on the Second Mesa had a chief named Maria Lanza, another great woman. Twylah Nitsch of the Seneca in New York is a wise and great woman. These are a few of many cases of great and brilliant women who were allowed to exercise their power and wisdom among their people. In some cases women became chiefs, medicine women, great singers, great poets, and storytellers. Some are well known for their art and basketmaking.

Respect for Mother Earth Begins with Respect for Women

We don't speak disrespectfully about women because respect for Mother Earth starts with respect for women. We have a great regard and respect for our women. It's even said in our meetings that the women are sacred and should be protected in their endeavors, while men are expendable. That's the importance our society attaches to women. The women are sacred because they can bring forth life, which no man can do.

It's said that no man would strike a woman except a coward, or if he were crazy or drunk. A man doesn't have to be jealous because it's the woman who's going to decide anyway who she wants to sleep with or marry. It's always the woman's choice and there is no need for a man to worry about it.

We don't overlook our women. They have a lot of power, important functions to fulfill, and plenty to say in our councils. Remember that wherever there is a wise man accomplishing anything, there's always a wise woman around too. That's the woman's power.

We get much guidance from our women and through their dreams as well. They have a way of thinking that men lack.

They are less aggressive, more compassionate, and wise in a way that men are not. Women tend to add a bit of knowledge at a critical time. Women are more intuitive than men; it's a highly developed protective instinct. Women can sometimes recognize what might have negative repercussions, and will bring this knowledge into play. This knowledge added to men's knowledge makes a completeness and a balance. Now, we men hate to admit such things, but it's true.

In certain tribes, and at particular meetings and places, it might appear as if the men run things. But you know what happened many times when we were dealing with a big problem and couldn't reach agreement? We would close the meeting and then go home and talk to our women. Then we'd come back and solve the problem.

Once in Stockholm I was at a meeting in a great hall full of people of all nationalities and political parties. The anarchists appeared to be sitting at the left, while the rightwing fanatics were on the right, and different ones of all types in the middle. About fifty of us Indians came in right down the middle, and we stood up to show them a picture of American Indian genocide that was smuggled out of Brazil. They were killing thousands of Indians and nobody gave a damn because they were just Indians.

In less than five minutes after it was shown, a leftwing person took the floor and a rightwing person responded, and soon they were involved in a real hot argument. That was the first time I had seen such arguments since I'd left America. I still didn't say anything; in certain places I like to be the last one to speak, but I had no idea what to say. I was standing right behind an Iroquois clan mother, and she softly said a few words. I don't think anyone else heard her. And the key was there for what had to be said, what had to be added. When I got up to speak I tried to make the walls of that hall shake, and I think I did. And they listened.

Women's Domains

The woman owns the house and everything in it. Once when I came home after working for the railroad, I found my belongings sitting outside the front door. According to our custom, I couldn't go in the house—it seemed as if I had been fired. I was standing there scratching my head and looking at my bedroll and rifle and everything sitting outside the door. I was shocked because my wife knew all my bad habits. She knew me better than anybody else, and I was trying to think about what I'd done wrong or what I hadn't done right. I couldn't think of what it was.

Then one of my daughters came running out. She was only about four or five years old then. But she said, "It's okay, Dad. You can come in the house. Mom said we're just cleaning house." So I crossed my fingers behind my back and threw my cap through the doorway into the house. When it didn't come flying back out at me, I knew it was okay to go in.

You see, if a man is abusive, doesn't provide, or whatever other reason, all the woman has to do to get rid of the man is to set his saddle, rifle, and bedroll outside the door. That's it. Yet, our men do not feel abused. It's said among my people that a man who doesn't have a woman doesn't deserve one. On the other hand, the women cannot be easily put aside. We know that women don't abuse their power, but that they use it to make us stronger.

In the old Indian society, our women had security, and so

did the children. If something happened to the father, all the children were wanted. The mother and her children could move in anywhere, and they were cared for. She could move in with her elder brother if the woman present, the first woman, approved of her. Or she could wait for another man to come along who pleased her. It was always the woman who had the last word. Security is the purpose of the tribe. Security is the interest of the chiefs, medicine people, and elders.

Having a clan mother—an older woman who knows and understands the people—is a good thing. It's the clan mother's responsibility to take care of the women, the home, and the men. Whenever a woman has a complaint, the clan mother is the one she goes to. Even when girls living in the city have trouble the clan mother knows. The clan mother is the first one to know if any of her girls are in trouble.

Men have to be careful. Once I made a girl cry. I thought I was correcting this young lady, and I guess I might have spoken kind of rough. After my wife, our clan mother, found out about it, I didn't do that again.

The women run the kitchen, and it happens that they do cook better. Sometimes if they're shorthanded the men help, but men can't go in there and fool around. One of our Indian rules is that when a man goes into the kitchen area, and he is not busy but only bothering the girls, the women have the authority to put an apron on him and he'll find himself cooking or washing dishes in a hurry. There's a certain order to these things.

In Indian society, women know the details about children's parents, who's married to whom, who goes with whom, who's related to whom, and all that. The oldest women in the tribe can always tell you who went with whom and for generations.

They are the ones that keep the tribal history by word of mouth. They tell the stories over and over so that they are not forgotten.

In the Indian way we don't have words for "bastard" or "stepchildren." There is no such thing as a bastard; why call little children or mothers names? I've met children and women who have been called these names. It's wrong, and makes me very angry.

Everyone is wanted. That's the way my wife and I raised our children: proud to be Indians and not to use dirty English such as stepfather or stepbrother. A woman shouldn't be ostracized if she has a baby out of marriage. Because Indian society has been upset, our culture partially destroyed and disrupted, we have more children born out of marriage than most groups, and more babies adopted out for either economic reasons or because the mothers can't take care of them.

Power of Grandmother Moon

The power of the Grandmother Moon is great. She watches over, guides, and affects women in many ways. At certain periods of the month women go off by themselves. A woman on her moon cycle is usually unhappy and negative, because when she starts her moontime she is being purified by nature of negative energy. That is why all ancient peoples had a lodge or little cabin where the woman could go and have peace of mind at that sacred time. This is mentioned even in the Christian bible. It shouldn't be looked upon with shame, but rather as a time of purification of a woman's mind, body, and spirit.

No men are permitted to enter the moon lodge or bother women at this time. The women are treated as queens; they remain in seclusion and get a lot of rest. It's a time of renewal. They are allowed to eat only potato soup, polenta, bananas, and other bland foods. Meat at this time is not permitted.

Not all Indians follow these customs nowadays, and many men have come to me with very bad backaches. Men and women who practice these customs are less neurotic and paranoid than people who do not. Men should not sleep with their women at this time of the month or even sit in a chair where a moon woman has sat. Separate rooms, and not just beds, are a good idea because being around moon women softens the flesh. White men suffer the same negative results regardless of their unnatural beliefs.

Women should not take part in ceremonies with other people during their moontimes. If they do, great confusion is likely, and people might start arguing and fighting among themselves. Women should not handle anyone else's feathers, pipes, or sacred objects because the medicines do not mix.

A woman's normal period between cycles should be about twenty-eight days, the same as the moon. After she has gone through the isolation period in the moon lodge, then she waits twenty-four hours after spotting in order to make sure she is done. Then she can come out, take a douche and bath, put on clean clothes, and rejoin the activities of everyone else.

Raising Children

Women as well as men should know that if you look at a baby and have a bad thought, the baby is likely to suffer the rest of its life. Swearing or saying bad things about a child is a terrible thing. When a mother or father tells a little child that it's bad, she's making that child bad.

You can put a curse on a little child. Children take being called names seriously, and it is the worst kind of swearing. So too it is that our minds should be kept clean, and adults should be very careful about words spoken to little children to avoid making them afraid.

When a baby is resting or sleeping in the crib, you should pray over the child in a good way. Tell him how good he is, how beautiful he is, how happy he is. You could even sing to babies while they sleep. Tell them the things they will be able to do in this life so they will have confidence. These prayers and songs will go into the baby's subconscious mind or spirit while he's lying there supposedly asleep.

Remember that whatever you are thinking about a child will go into her, and it will come back to you later when the child becomes a teenager. The child will get even with you later if you screamed at her, spoke to her in an unkind way, swore at her, or beat her up. If you treat children in these ways, they could grow up to be bums—they will turn on you, and possibly even rob you.

We raise our children differently. Everyone in the camp helps watch out for the children. The children start out learning respect for the animals and other forms of life around them. They learn to grow up with respect for other people. Children should be raised from birth not to be allowed to do anything and everything they want to do, such as kicking the cat, or drawing a fist to parents or other elders.

I think all children should have pets. My kids had bobcats raised in the house and a crow that lived outside. They had all manner of pets, and by learning respect for the animals they also learned respect for each other.

I see children nowadays interrupting their elders when

they are talking just like it was nothing. I was taught to stand back, wait my turn, and then to ask my question very quietly. But now children are raised where both father and mother have to work to maintain expensive homes. You can't force somebody to do something when they don't want to do it. Civilized people believe too much in this element of force, and that's what's going to turn on them.

We had a little red schoolhouse for a while at Meta Tantay and it worked out beautifully; the kids loved it. They were taken for nature walks every day out in the sagebrush. They learned to understand the snakes, coyotes, eagles, owls, the many birds. They learned what they were here for, what their job was to keep things in balance. Little children, third or fourth graders, were making scale models of tractors, buses, and telegraph machines that worked. In a school like this the kids will be interested and they will learn. Then you will have intelligent people later who could invent anything that's needed. Such people would not pollute or destroy because they would love what they were doing.

On Marriage and Sex

Another thing that's very bad is arguing in front of the children. I've never had to live like that, so I don't understand why people should act shameful. When we followed our Indian ways, we got along very well. Families were very close and everyone was very respectful of each other. There's not supposed to be arguing and fighting in the home. I was told a long time ago by an old man that when I got angry, or if my woman got angry, I should take a walk, go fishing, come back later, and it would be all right.

Many Indians have become too civilized. When people don't get along with their own families, when there is jealousy and anger, it's because they were corrupted. It might have been the missionaries, or because they were adopted out or sent off to boarding schools.

Love in our way is not merely a sex thing, and it's not merely a thing between two people who claim to own each other. It's nothing like the civilized way of making false promises, daring to do what you think the other one shouldn't do, signing a paper to make it legal, paying some money, and then letting the contest start. It's not this possession kind of thing— what I call an ownership complex—where you have to have a contract and might even get to consider yourselves each other's jailers. The attitude toward each other under these conditions is not peaceful, and maybe that's why people get to a point that they get so mean in general, even with each other.

In the Indian way we say that when we get married we have a good understanding. It's a beautiful ceremony where the whole village forms a big circle. Then the couple has to be led by the medicine man through the four stages of life, and he explains all of it so they have an understanding of what it's about. We say that we have a good understanding, and that one person does not harm the other. We're very serious about something that sacred: it has to be a thing of beauty, not anger, selfishness, or greed. Then the children grow up well adjusted in the traditional way of life and don't have all the problems.

I like to perform Indian weddings. All the young man's and young woman's relations are there. The last part is where I whip out a razor-sharp knife and cut the veins of both of them so as to mix the blood. Then I tie them together with a piece of buckskin string. It's a beautiful thing.

In the Indian way, people don't get married on the spur of the moment like modern people do. Maybe the young man has to take horses, blankets, different things to the woman's parents. He has to show he's capable, and that he can take care of the woman. And so too the young lady has to show that she is ready and capable. She has to make a pair of moccasins and then take them to the old grandma or clan mother. The clan mother's gonna turn them wrong side out and look at the stitches. Then the young lady has to cook a meal that the man likes.

The young man takes the horses or blankets, maybe a few more each day until they're taken inside of the woman's parents' corral. That's the sign of acceptance, and so the old people do have something to say about it, but in all this process, it's the woman who has the final say in everything.

When I was a young man and I first met my wife in a cafe, I had three girls with me at the time. I fed them because I'm a gentleman and then let them go. I came back two days later and she was there. I know she hadn't been there all that time, but she was in the right place at the right time and I proposed to her. I immediately took her out on the sidewalk and asked her if she could cook. She said she could. And I said, "Let's go home." I was hungry and needed a woman.[1]

Regarding sex, there was a time with the Christians that everything having to do with sex was dirty or nasty. In the Indian way, sex is part of nature, and considered a natural function for people, and must be treated with respect. It was not pornography nor evil. People were healthy and had healthy minds. That's why we didn't have a lot of so-called sexual problems that a lot of modern people are having.

In our communities men are proud to be men and women are proud to be women. There is a respect, a balance of things in which no one takes advantage of their own position. In Meta Tantay, everything had to go by Indian tribal rules. Some girls worked in the gardens, and some liked to help take care of the animals. The girls were never allowed to do the heavy work where they might hurt themselves. Heavy, dangerous work is relegated to the men, such as using chain saws, or lifting cross ties or huge rocks. The women also dug a cellar, and I was opposed to that and was called a male chauvinist. The men still wouldn't let the ladies put the heavy timbers into place. So it's not a matter of discrimination, but rather what the person likes to do, is qualified for, and can do best.

I'm a rough old man and old-fashioned. When the ladies go to town with me they wear a long dress. I don't see anything wrong with wearing a dress. In this cold climate I don't say they have to, but I noticed that even the Eskimo women in Alaska, dressed head to foot in fur, had a little skirt to indicate that they were women and proud of it.

When our people are raised in a healthy environment, they don't have women liberation problems. Women's liberation was already a fact among Native Americans before Columbus or any other illegal immigrants had become a fact of life and law of the land.

I'm an optimist. I see our families and our tribes coming back together. I see others doing the same thing, and I think that's good. We like to see families coming together, people learning how to work together, pray together, and do things together just like our tribes did in the past.

Understand too that the word "love" is misused in modern society. True love is a love of life, of all nature and all beautiful things that were put here for our benefit. True love extends to Mother Earth, Father Sun, Grandmother Moon, stars in the sky that guide our way and give us messages, all animal life, plant life, bird life, and people of different tribes, nationalities, and races. I hope I've given you a little clue or hint of true love and of how to better your own life. *Ho.*

NOTE

1. In reality, Rolling Thunder did not make a sudden decision regarding his own marriage. A year or two prior to his encounter with Spotted Fawn in the cafe, he had a vision during which he was shown the woman he would marry. See "Visiting Hell" section in chapter 7.

CHAPTER FIVE

Rolling Thunder on speaking tour in Europe, 1982.

A Medicine Man's Rx

*"I can reach far more people by teaching people
how to heal themselves than I can by doing the
work myself just one at a time."*

The last time I was in the Bay area the people there were angry. They used to be healthy, friendly people, but now they're angry. Somebody asked me why I thought they were angry. I said that I didn't know the exact reasons, but that if I had to live in that kind of environment and drink filthy recycled water, and breathe the lead in the air like those people have to, I'd be angry too.

It's part of our religion to be healthy in body and mind. When you feel good and you have a healthy body and a healthy mind, you don't want to destroy anything, and you don't hate anyone. The spiritual part comes first, and then health of body and mind.

Origins of Modern Medicine

There's not that much difference between medicine men and medical doctors because the medicine of both came from the same place. If you don't think so, take a look at the medical doctor symbol, a cross with two snakes wrapped around it. I've asked many people about the meaning of those two snakes, and not too many could tell me because they've lost their original teachings. The snakes meant healing and wisdom.

We know the snake is the most powerful of all creatures. We use the snake in our medicine, and in the ancient times we used snake venom when we operated on the brain. When used right, a certain amount of snake venom constricts the blood vessels and deadens pain. Medical doctors learned how to perform brain surgery a few years ago, but it was done here ten thousand years ago.

Modern medicine started mainly with herbs and herbal extracts from American Indians. Many herbs, like Mormon tea, are misnamed. The Indians taught the Mormons how to use that plant. A great many of the "modern" medicines, like aspirin, are not new inventions. Originally aspirin came from white willow bark. Quinine came from this land too, not from across the ocean. Penicillin originally came from the mold on the oak log. My father told me how it was when they were raided and they'd get shot. They'd take the mold off the oak log, grind it up, put it in water, and drink it. They would take honey or a cactus pad and smash it up, soak a silk handkerchief with the liquid, and then pull it through wounds. The wounds would heal, and sometimes with no scars. They even had ways of curing a crushed (not broken) leg.

Many of our medicines were hidden to preserve them, because war is still being made on us, our people are molested, our medicine and our way of life ridiculed, and we are called witch doctors. The best of our medicines have been put away until they can be brought out at the right time. When the time comes, we will be glad to *share,* not give away. Why don't we make it public? For whose benefit? So we can be ripped off again? Or so that the medicines are misused only for profit and greed, and not made available to the poor people who need them? When we talk about sharing, we're not talking about one-sided sharing. We don't do good for evil. Yet there's no price to our knowledge. We don't set any price except justice and freedom for all when the day comes that we Indians are recognized as people.

A doctor from New York wrote to me saying that he'd like to come and visit and see how I put my medicines together "for the benefit of posterity." Ha! I didn't like the sound of it. So I answered his letter and told him I realized whose posterity he was talking about and not to bother to come out to Carlin.

I know there have been teams looking for cures for cancer, roaming the jungles, going among different Indian tribes up and down the Americas. They sent a team of eight medical people to the Navajo reservation trying to find out why Navajo Indians never have cancer. Actually, they do have cancer, but they know how to take care of it.

As new diseases came along in this land—cancers, syphilis, leprosy, and the black plague—at first we traditional healers couldn't cope with them because they were foreign, new to us. But we can cope with most things today, even though most progress in Indian medicine was stopped because it was forced underground. Native healers have gone to jail for practicing what they know. I guess the medical doctors don't want competition. In our world, the competition that worries medical doctors does not exist.

There is nothing, and I mean nothing, that can't be cured. For instance, wherever you go and there is a sickness, a cure would be nearby, and it might be what some people call a weed. If there are poisonous snakes in the swamp, nearby would be a plant that will cure the snake bite. Maybe the modern doctors and scientists ought to go to Africa and talk with some old medicine man over there about a cure for AIDS. I've had cases of leprosy, rabies, cancer, and AIDS sent to me by doctors, but they have to keep it quiet.

A few years ago a modern medical person went to China and "discovered" acupuncture. Of course, the Chinese people have a long history and culture, and had been practicing acupuncture for a very long time. But then because someone went to China and watched an operation in which the patient had no pain, suddenly it was decided that acupuncture wasn't superstition, that it did work.

The American Medical Association wouldn't like it if I opened an office somewhere. In fact, I don't have any paper to hang on the wall or card to carry in my wallet to prove anything, and I wouldn't take it if somebody gave it to me. We don't look to any foreign governments and nobody has authority except the Great Spirit. No one has a monopoly on the Great Spirit's way of life, and no one has a monopoly on healing—they just think they do.

I'm sorry for the medical profession. They've got far more problems than we medicine men. Not too long ago barbers were called on to perform operations. Barbers were surgeons and they performed surgery in the barber chair. Now the modern medical doctors don't tell you that because it's kind of embarrassing for them. They're afraid they might be ostracized, or there might be someone who says they don't know all there is to know.

In the mid-1970s I met with a past president of the AMA and he and I started off on the wrong foot. Some of my doctor friends invited me to meet the old gentleman, but he was kind of stubborn and blockheaded, and I think he didn't know who he was talking to. When he started with this poor Indian stuff— "Too bad what happened to the poor Indians," "You Indians need more education," phony sympathy and crocodile tears— I told him a few things. When I got through with him I think we had a better understanding of each other.

I told him the Incas were practicing brain surgery more than ten thousand years ago and the same thing was being done all over this country. I explained to him the techniques and how it was done, what we used for anesthetic, what we used to stop the flow of blood and kill the pain. He looked amazed and shocked. Then he went over to the bar and poured himself a tall glass of gin, and sat down in a corner and sulked for a while. The other doctors and I talked about different medical things, and had a fine time and fine conversation. Finally, this old boy forgot himself and joined in. When I left, I shook his hand and told him I'd had a wonderful time talking to him, and that he wasn't as ignorant as he was pretending to be.

It makes me feel real bad sometimes when I have to turn people down, but I am not responsible for the stupid laws. For example, chemotherapy might save some lives, but why should we have to take this very dangerous treatment when we have our own better treatment? Many people are victims of the stupid laws brought here and placed on top of us. I've always had a dream of a clinic or hospital where American Indian healing would be legal again. It would be a clinic where we could all work together in our own way to help people. In other words, in this type of clinic you would find acupuncture people, healers of different kinds, and doctors too.

Once a group in California offered to raise funds using my name, and they said they would build a clinic. Of course, they would retain ownership of the land and the buildings, but I would be "permitted" to go there. Mind the language now, that's the way the letter read. I would be permitted to go there, and a laboratory would be set up to analyze my medicines to see if they worked. I am going to ask them to prove things that we've known for ten thousand years or more? I have not asked anyone to prove anything to me because I'm not busy proving anything myself.

It was like offering me a dream on the one hand, and on the other hand, saying that "we are going to take the gravy, we are going to steal what you people know, we're going to take it and make a lot of money, and you Indians can go chase yourselves." That's the way it's always been. In order for us to share more of our medicine knowledge, non-Indians need to show their good intentions by giving a little bit of the land back. If they cannot, then sharing is never going to be possible. If the Indians aren't on their own land and feel at home when they're there, to hell with it.

I know some people think medicine men ought to be fanatical like many of the doctors, but we're not. We have to keep an open mind because we get more cures that way. Nowadays we are glad we have doctors. They have medicines that will fix up patients in a minute; they are better at some things than we are, and one of these things is surgery. American Indians could once perform brain surgery and cure crushed limbs. But that was many years ago, and we have been out of practice now a long time because of stupid, repressive laws. We live under a dictatorship and are very limited in what we can do and avoid going to jail. I have never had a desire to be a martyr or die for somebody else's stupid mistakes or stupid laws.

There is good and bad in all things, and you have to understand that and apply it. For instance, I don't know the correct word in high English for a blood clot in the leg, but I think it's much better when you can use a plastic vein to splice in and remove the clot. I've heard some people say they don't believe in splicing and using plastic, but in that case I say it's good. If it saves the man's leg I think it's much superior to cutting off his leg merely because of the blood clot.

Not everything that doctors support is bad. Nowadays they make some herbal medicines synthetically where the herb is condensed down, put into pill form, and is easier to handle. It's mighty hard to go out and gather herbs in the winter, especially when there's snow on the ground. I've done it, but not everyone's going to do it. Anyway, when you have it there handy to use, modern methods are sometimes good.

Some things to watch out for are x-rays, antibiotics, and metal fillings. X-rays should be given only by a qualified technician, and frequent x-rays avoided. Antibiotics should be used with caution because they kill the natural bacteria in the stomach. You have to take something to counter strong herbs that kill natural bacteria as well; I like prune juice as a counter. If you have metal fillings in your teeth, you should have them replaced with plastic ones.

Of course, I don't think it's natural to cut organs out, or slice up a person like a piece of bologna. Heart and kidney transplants are something else again. A little bit of the other person's soul goes into the patient; perhaps the other person was wicked.

The main theme for healing in terms of our religion is respect. Some years ago a large group of friends of a young lady who had been in a terrible car accident wanted me to see her in the hospital in San Raphael. She was unconscious, broken up really bad, and they were going to put her in a mental institution. They said she was going to be a vegetable for the rest of her life if she lived. What happened was that they had moved her after the accident. She was lying on the highway; the ambulance came and they moved her quickly to the hospital miles away. We medicine men know that when people suffer trauma, and are unconscious while they are moved, the spirit comes back and cannot find the body. I took care of that young girl and she became a beautiful woman and a teacher. The spiritual as well as the physical must always be considered.

Maybe someday certain people will get together and start to change some of the silly laws and ignorant attitudes that long ago should have been changed. Pretty soon everyone is going to be in the same boat as the Indians, priced out of medical care. When I visited Alaska with the Eskimos, I found out that they had been cut off from all medical aid. They wouldn't fly the Eskimos to the hospital in Anchorage even if they were dying. I walked in the woods with them and found that many of the old ones still knew a lot of their original herbal medicines, even for cancer. The Eskimos had no choice but to turn back to their own traditional medicines.

On Pure Water, Food, and Air

Live water is water before it's had poisons and chemicals added to it. If we drink dead water or eat dead food, we're not nourishing our bodies. It isn't going to do anything for us. There are many herbs and minerals that could be added to water and food; using dangerous poisons is not necessary.

Water is the greatest purifier. According to our health code water is sacred; whenever we take a drink, we always give thanks. It is supposed to be pure to flush and purify the body, and be kept pure for use in cooking and medicine. If you drink filthy water that somebody has taken a crap in upstream or recycled sewer water with poisonous chemicals added to it, the mind is going to be affected. Everyone should know that. Do you have to analyze it in chemistry laboratories and prove it before you can believe it?

Drinking water in some places contains formaldehyde and about thirty-two other chemicals to clean it up. Using these chemicals is not necessary. I found a way to purify my water in town; it needs purifying because they put chemicals in it. I used a filter, but I could still smell the chlorine and the dead germs. I have a powerful sense of smell, and if it isn't right, I know it. So I boil my water, and place a few fresh bay leaves in the water. They are a great water purifier, germ stopper, and antibiotic. I boil them right in with the water and put in a little sassafras. It smells good and thins the blood, and is good for the heart. These herbs give the water a golden color. The water then tastes like pure water, and the bay leaves and sassafras counter chemicals and dead germs.

Spraying insects is bad too because it taints the water and kills off the fish. I teach people to take a spoonful of apple cider vinegar two or three times a day and leave the sugar alone through the mosquito season. But they're modern and don't want to give up sugar, so that's their own karma. After all, those little mosquitoes have to eat too, but not by me. They should be fed by the sugar eaters, not me.

We have to eat good food to stay healthy. Our health code gave us extensive guidance, and one thing that's very important is to pray over the food before eating it. Pray over your food and watch the effects. We pray over the tame animals even and make an offering when they are slaughtered to show our appreciation and thankfulness, and to tell them the good way in which they are going to be used. We pray over the food when it's cooked, and even the vegetables when they are harvested. We show our appreciation in this way so that the food will be medicine, easily digestible and nourishing. We are also supposed to pray over food to cleanse it of any invisible evil spirits that might be in it.

I don't agree with spraying plants and using commercial fertilizers, and then adding more chemicals for preservatives. Such preservatives only add more poisons. I always look at the labels on food, and the longer the name of the ingredient and the more of them, I figure that's a sign to stay away. There are other ways of preserving food. Dead food will not nourish you. The life in food is also killed by radiation and using microwave ovens.

My elder advised me to be sure to *exhale* but not *inhale* when I go to a big city. Polluted air affects the body and the mind. I've seen people in those big cities who never had a breath of fresh air nor a drink of pure water in their entire lives. Most of those people are pretty dragged out.

We don't need anything that destroys the mind or body. The liver is the most important organ in the body. Some people think it's the heart, but the liver cleans out the body, purifies it, so that's where most of the sickness starts from. I don't think people realize the harm that so many of these chemicals in the water, food, and air can do to the body and the mind.

The great majority of people, young and elderly, are half dead. I have a very difficult time getting new ideas, strange ideas, through to them. Their minds have become conditioned and regimented, but there's something else at work here. It could be that a large degree of it is living in the middle of a concrete city and taking continual overdoses of these chemicals. The reason for the deterioration of health and well-being of most people is the pollution of the air, water, and the environment itself, and failing to understand nature and how these things affect them.

The doctors and gurus should tell them these things because they are supposed to be teachers as well as doctors waiting for someone to get sick so they can make money. Legislation should be signed to protect people and not force even more chemicals and poisons on them. It's not up to me to tell non-Indian people where they should start—county, state, or federal level. That's their politics, but it should be done. I'm certain there are people who have the responsibility and the intelligence to get started. But some people are so dead, so apathetic, that I don't look for many to even write a letter to their representatives. I don't look for many to do anything about anything, except sit and wait for some spiritual experience to come to them. They're gonna be waiting an awful long time.

When pollution starts destroying plant and animal life, you don't have to use your imagination too much to understand the harm it's doing to people. It's going to take an awful lot of purification of mind and body before these things can be cleaned up. People cannot avoid all pollution these days. People should be watchful and cleanse themselves more often to purify their bodies and try to survive as best they can. That's why our purification ceremonies are more necessary than ever before.

Destroying nature and people with it is an evil thing. I hope that people who don't deserve it don't suffer. But if people have been sitting back and don't care what happens to the Indians or don't care what happens to nature, then why in hell should I or the Great Spirit care for them? Our ways are not the do good for evil kind.

Nutrition Prescriptions and Proscriptions

I can only eat "ethnic" food, that is, original, healthy kinds that are both food and medicine. We say "healthy food," rather than health food, and there is a difference. If you want to know what healthy food is, and you didn't ask your doctor or highly trained nutritionists, maybe I can tell you.

Trace your ancestry back seven generations—the number seven always comes into play in anything that has life. Trace it back as far as you can, whatever your ethnicity, and see what they ate. It takes seven generations to accustom the body to a new kind of food. Now I know a lot of people want to pump you up and make you feel good, and they're going to tell you it doesn't make any difference. Well, maybe they say that because they don't know; it does make a difference, especially physically. For instance, when Asian people come here they have to have a little rice; otherwise, they won't be healthy. For Scandinavian people it takes a little fish each day, and Puerto Rican people need beans and rice. We American Indians need meat.

American Indians require just a little meat each day according to how cold it is, and how hard the person is working. The government knew that when they ordered the killing off of the buffalo, took away hunting rights from the Indians, and first issued beef after the Indians were penned up in concentration camps on the reservation. Later on the Indians ate whatever they could get because they were hungry. The sugar issued to them was very harmful. Government issue coffee was also harmful compared to the natural herbal teas. There were many other harmful foods provided to the Indians, unnatural things, including dairy products and butter, that could form cholesterol and lead to gallstones and heart attacks.

I'm not apologizing for the fact that we eat meat. We think we're just as good as vegetarians. One mistake I see vegetarians make is they fail to recognize that, like the Mother Earth, plants have living bodies and are also living beings. A vegetarian diet might be all right for some people, except that sometimes you might not get enough protein. I know some of the vegetarians won't agree with me, but I won't argue with them. In any case, we believe in a balance.

We know the Great Spirit put certain animals here for part of our food, and to be used in a right way. But we're not fanatical. I've known some good vegetarians and they're really nice people. When we came to visit they would feed us bean sprouts, lettuce, nuts, and maybe a little cheese. Not to accept their food would have been an insult in our way, but later we'd go out and order a big steak somewhere. We don't say we're better than those people who prefer to be vegetarians. What's good for one person is not necessarily good—or may even be poisonous—to another, and that applies to both medicine and food. Some doctors and nutrition experts don't take into account individual considerations.

I use food as medicine, but I have to go way back to my original food and Indian cooking. Buffalo meat cooked in the old way is marinated; it comes out so tender you can cut it with a spoon, and there is no fat. The trouble is that when you eat buffalo cooked in this way you'll never like beef again, because it is greasy and shot through with hormones. The poor cows, they're about bred out and they're so dumb. We say we become like what we put into our bodies, and if we eat buffalo we're going to be like an old buffalo. If we eat deer, we're going to be like that deer, and if we eat dumb cow, well, just look at the faces of some of those big cattlemen who eat their own meat. At Meta Tantay, we raised most of our own meat, and it's good when raised without chemicals or additives and killed in the proper way.

The American diet causes diabetes and other problems, including prostate and kidney diseases. Modern medical people want to pretend they don't know where these diseases come from, and maybe they don't. But I know where they come from: civilized food and civilized eating habits.

American eating habits are bad, and in Europe I found them a bit worse. They didn't like it when I would tell them how to change their diet to eat better and cheaper. Everything we put into our bodies is live water or dead water, and live food or dead food. If we put dead food in our bodies, it's not nourishing. If we put live, organic food into our bodies, then we can be healthy. Because spiritual health is related to physical health, we don't want to load our bodies with more chemicals and unhealthy foods than our bodies can compensate for.

Even though some Indians get addicted to pork, it's not original to this land. If anyone wants to get over arthritis, one of the first things to do is not eat pork. Traditional Indians do not eat bacon or other forms of pork. Beef is not very good and is not as digestible as buffalo or deer meat. Sheep meat is good, and goat meat is good and digestible. If you are not a meat eater, then do so with moderation and wisdom. Pick poultry and fish. Fish is good and digestible.

In civilized society we don't get enough natural animal or

fish oils to lubricate our bodies anymore. We need this oil in order to hold in suspension the other things that can cause gallstones and cholesterol. You know your automobile needs oil; all moving machinery needs oil. So I don't understand how it is that modern people ever got the idea they do not need oil. When people don't get enough oil, they get arthritis, rheumatism, and their brains clog up; worst of all, their sex organs clog up while they're still young.

Fish oil is one of the best types of oil. We don't eat butter, imitation or otherwise. Imitation butter has some of the same chemical components as butter. Milk, butter, and dairy products cause cholesterol in the veins, and then heart attacks. Yogurt and kumiss are good, but we keep most dairy products out of our systems. I'd like to take health food faddists to the cleaners. People have been sold a bill of goods being told that to be healthy, they should drink milk everyday. Healthy food is not health food.

Fruits are good, with the exception of bananas. They are picked green and then artificially ripened. They are very constipating, and also bad for anyone with asthma. One banana now and then is okay. We don't use sugar of any kind, including brown sugar. We do allow honey in moderation.

I quit drinking coffee because it's bad for the liver. Now I drink only natural herbal teas. Prune juice is good and helps the stomach stay in shape—no ulcers. Grapefruit juice is good to help digest meat. Since I quit coffee my prostate and kidney troubles cleared up real fast. Watermelon is also very good for the kidneys.

Modern people seem to have forgotten that greens are good to eat. I'm talking about greens rather than salad. Salads are hard to digest, especially if you're sick. A bit of salad might be all right from time to time, but some people overdo it. For sick people with a weak stomach, salad should be a no-no.

Greens cooked and fried in oil, like we Cherokees do, are delicious. The greens, onion tops, and mushrooms are all cooked kind of like a Chinese stir fry. All the flavor is saved and the vitamins are not destroyed if they are cooked on slow heat. The vitamins go into the oil and water and are not lost.

Bread is one of the worst starchy things you can eat. I want you to get the message clearly: I didn't say one type of bread, but rather breads of all kinds. Starch in bread and in potatoes is like beef fat—it's indigestible. Peanut butter and cheese also clog people up.

My instincts guide me about certain chemicals. Watch out especially for monosodium glutamate. Cornstarch works just as well as MSG. It's almost impossible to find quality food that's not loaded with chemicals. The only thing you can do about it is to raise your own and read the labels on food.

When you start making changes in your diet, at first you might think you'll starve to death. Well, that's good too. You need to fast a little while, but no more than seven days at a time. Then you'll find there are so many other things that you can eat. But nothing will work if you continue to take drugs, alcohol, or chemicals in your food.

ROLLING THUNDER'S DIET

Breakfast

1 cup hot prune juice   *2 poached eggs*
1 slice toast   *Yogurt*
Small bowl of stewed prunes   *Greens cooked thoroughly*
Beans in their broth

Lunch

Beans in their broth
Beets
Soup

Chicken or turkey
Greens

Dinner

Beans in broth
Beef stew or fish
Asparagus

Cooked cabbage
Fruit (peaches, figs, plums,
    watermelon, pineapple)

Drinks

Cranberry juice
Orange juice
Apple juice

Prune juice
Grapefruit juice
Herbal teas

Condiments

Raw onion
Raw garlic
Apple cider or rice vinegar
Mustard

Horseradish
Olive, safflower, or
    sunflower oil

Good vegetables

Nettles
Kale
Yams (not sweet
    potatoes)
Carrots
Endive
Squash (all kinds)
Dandelion greens
Avocados
Red beets
Spinach
Turnips

Cabbage
Broccoli
Bok choy
Cauliflower
Celery (cooked or
    raw, good for
    nerves)
Asparagus (cleans
    out kidneys)
Salads (wash all
    ingredients with
    vinegar and
    water)

Cucumber
Artichokes
Onions (to purify
    the blood)
Garlic (antibiotic)
Cactus (immune
    system booster)
Greens (turnip,
    mustard, beet,
    dandelion)

Soups

Always use organic chicken or beef broth as a base

Avoid

Cheese	*Jams and jellies*
Butter	*Bread (of any kind,*
MSG	*especially white; small*
Pork	*amounts only)*
Coffee (regular or	*Potatoes, pasta, and other*
decaffeinated)	*starches (small amounts*
Soda (regular or diet)	*only)*
Sugar (treat it like poison)	

On Herbal Medicine

We have medicines so powerful, so strong, that one seed too many will kill you. I've had people come to me and say that they want to learn about the herbs in a week. Well, it takes twenty or thirty years in our training, and then you have to know what you are doing to tell someone to take something for their benefit.

I use over a thousand herbs. I don't know how many exactly because I don't count them. Out of the millions of herbs, "civilized" society has classified only about 500,000 with Latin names, and of these, they know only a little of what about 10,000 of them do. I don't make claims that I know all about herbs. There's a new one every year. People ask me to name them, and I don't know the names. There are thousands, and I couldn't tell you the English names even if you asked me. The names don't impress me anyway, so I know very few of the Latin or English names for herbs.

When I need a medicine I go out and I'll find it. I can talk to an herb, hold it in my hand, and know in a few minutes what that herb is here for, what its purpose is. I try to get herbs that grow in a particular area.

I talk about only so much at a time, so people listening to me don't go out and hurt someone; I know how people can misinterpret things. There are always two plants that look alike— one will be good and the other deadly poison. After three drops of an herb I know, a person can no longer speak. Maybe certain politicians should get a dose of this herb.

Herbs should be respected and handled very carefully. An example is another little plant that grows out on the desert. It grows about three inches high, and one drop of the juice will choke you to death in a few minutes. So you learn from the old ones. I don't advise anyone to go stomping out in the woods and yanking up the medicine. It can be dangerous unless you're an expert. I advise people to go to their local herb store where you can get some of the herbs known to be harmless, as well as herbs that are not so powerful. There's no objection to using herbs as long as you know what you're doing, and you can't hurt yourself or anyone else. When herbs are used in a right way, then they're good.

Each individual has different requirements. That's why I don't write overall prescriptions for herbs. In *Back to Eden*[1] you can find really good material on the use of herbs. I would also like to explain about plant life. When I gather plants for my medicine—and I gather some real powerful ones—I gather them so that they stay powerful. Somebody else might go out there and start yanking them up, but then the plants will do nothing for them and perhaps even poison them.

I gather my plants between sunrise and sunset only, never

at nighttime. At nighttime we let them sleep and rest. The plants have a life, a tribe, a family, and a chief, just like we do. I find the chief and sing to him, and I never take the chief or any of his ladies around him. I have a way of knowing which ones are good for what sickness, which ones are poisonous, and which one is the chief. I don't know if I could explain it in English. When I gather medicine I have to make an offering. Nothing is really free, especially if it contains life. I make an offering of tobacco, beads, or something else, and a prayer, an apology.

Plants have the same kind of order of things, only they can communicate on a much higher level. They don't have to make a lot of noise when they communicate, but they know what's happening. They can read our thoughts. I've seen some plants fold their leaves in fear when certain people approach them. I like to see the plants happy, and I explain to them in my prayers how they're gonna be used in a good way, and that they should be happy for what they're doing. I explain in my prayers that they need not fear, and that we won't take too much, never more than half. Sometimes when I gather herbs, the bees will move back because they know I'll only take so much and leave some for them.

If I only see one or two plants, I let them be to reproduce. That's our reverence for plant life. I don't believe in killing plants or destroying them. If I take some roots from below the ground, then I have to smooth the dirt back just like it was and maybe replant a seed or a piece of the root so that the plant can grow again.

When I go out to gather herbs I gather enough to last the winter. I dry them in the shade so they'll keep their natural juices and stay green after they're dry.

You will find that there are seven different things that each plant does well. You'll find seven side effects that you have to compensate for in some way. The number seven is in all of what you might call "magic," but it's in the physical too. The number seven always applies in medicine or what you call "religion."

The most beneficial of the herbs we have are outlawed, off the market completely. The state of Nevada went all out: even if you consult with your own family and tell them to take these herbs, they could put you in jail. Now the federal government is trying to pass laws to match some of these fanatical state laws. They even took chaparral—which had been used successfully for centuries against cancer—off the market.[2]

It seems as if civilized society is not interested in making things better, but rather in anything for the dollar. When they look at a tree, they think of so many board feet of lumber worth so many dollars. When I look at a tree, I think about how beautiful that tree is. I look at so-called weeds in same way. You ought to see my yard. In the summertime it's like a jungle in the middle of the desert. The plants know they're wanted; when I need a certain kind of medicine, a new plant comes to live here. No botany experts could identify them. I had to name them myself. Maybe they weren't born yet or in my yard before, but they know they're wanted. They know when they are wanted, just like people know where they're welcomed. In other words, it's good to be wanted.

I catch people's thinking sometimes, and some have wondered if I smoke pot. We medicine men don't smoke marijuana. We smoke a different plant used for purification, to make the mind feel good. I'm not here to run marijuana down. It's not as harmful as booze, heroin, cocaine, or those pills made out of chemicals, but don't expect me to lie to you. Marijuana is a downer; if a person is already depressed, then it's very bad for them. I'm not fanatical either, and I'm not saying pot and some other stuff doesn't do any good. It might in some cases of hypertension. People are under a lot of stress nowadays.

When used in a medicine way marijuana is good. It was used in the old days to cure stomach ulcers and glaucoma in the eyes, but not to smoke. It's not that there is anything wrong with marijuana; there might be something wrong with the people who think they have to use it. To use marijuana or any kind of drug in that kind of way is not good. There are ways of getting vibes and energy that are more powerful than any drugs or booze.

Did you ever smell the air just after the lightning flash? How good it smells with the ozone in the air? Inhale that air real deeply, and then you'll understand how good it makes you feel. Catch a cup of the thunder water that comes down just after the lightning flashes. Drink that water, get as high as you want, and you'll see how much more energy you have. This thunder water is charged by the lightning and it's just like charging a battery when you drink it. But you'll still know what's going on around you and not be stupid. Great Spirit wants us to stand up with clear minds like men and women should.

A lot of people are so greedy they go out and take the magic mushroom or peyote or devil weed. They might have a good trip, and they might have three. They might even have up to seven, if they're lucky. But that seventh one is going to kill them because they are not going to desecrate our sacred medicine. Nine young people in California read those Don Juan books, so they went out with that big shot attitude and took what they call devil weed, jimson weed. They took it all by themselves with no teacher, no guide. Not one of them got away: three went crazy, three went blind, and three died.

In the pipe we sometimes smoke tobacco mixed with certain herbs that bring peace of mind and calm the person down. But it's not good when these things are used just to get high with. Tobacco is sacred to us. This land is where it came from, but now there are twenty-one chemicals in the cigarettes people smoke, and one causes impotence. Certain people in civilized society want to blame the tobacco. They don't blame the chemicals. Isn't that strange? It doesn't make sense to me that politicians pass strict laws against marijuana, which in itself is quite harmless compared to some of the chemicals they allow in the water and food all the time.

Medicines, Potions, and Teas

Here are a few helpful things so that you don't need to run to a doctor every time you get a cold. But you'll have to figure out the dose yourself or ask your doctor because I don't prescribe anything. I have to say too for the benefit of my own protection that if the condition continues to persist, see your own physician.

HOW TO MAKE HERBAL TEAS

Boil one gallon of good water in a large pot, and then take the pot off the heat. Put herbs in water and let steep for one hour. Do not boil the herbs. Strain and store balance of the tea in the refrigerator until ready to use again. Reheat when needed.

Alternatively, in the summer you can put the herbs in a wide-mouth gallon jug with water and place it out in the sun. This is the best way to make herbal teas. Strain, store, and refrigerate until needed.

Teas are most effective when warm and taken on an empty stomach. Drink one cup at the following times: in the morning before breakfast, 30 minutes before lunch, 30 minutes before dinner, and 30 minutes before bed. Always pray over the tea first to give it direction.

NOTE: *Do not use aluminum pots to make or store teas.*

MEDICINE FOR HIGH AND LOW BLOOD SUGAR

In the first place, you should stay away from sugar. Compensate for it with something else, such as honey. Take a little every time you feel a low blood sugar attack coming on. Take a bit of Jerusalem artichokes—they didn't come from Jerusalem, but rather from the country where the Cherokees originated—for their natural insulin.

Both cedar and juniper berries are very good for working against sugar diabetes. Grind the berries and make a tea. Drink it by the cupful as often as needed, and make it as strong as you want. It's all right to add a little something for flavor, like lemon grass or chamomile, as well as a bit of honey. The best time to drink the tea is when you're feeling kind of cross, maybe confused in the mind, and your energy is kind of low. If you feel it coming on, don't wait for it to happen. The quicker you drink the tea, the better. Don't wait until you get to feeling real bad. There's a tendency to magnify things in the mind when this happens and to need someone to blame, so start right in. This tea works for both high and low blood sugar.

There are also herbs that help stimulate the glands so there will be enough of the chemical the body uses to manufacture insulin. One of them is gentian root.

MEDICINE FOR AIDS AND CANCER

The prepared cacti called "nopalitos" contain chromium, which boosts the immune system. Yucca also contains lots of chromium and is helpful for AIDS patients. You can buy nopalitos in supermarkets; I think all AIDS patients should be eating cactus. Then I'd use echinacea root, which stops infections of all kinds. I also use calcium, magnesium, and zinc. These are good against all kinds of sickness. Zinc is especially good against the common cold.

Chaparral is a well-known herb used against cancer, as well as AIDS, and many other communicable diseases. AIDS patients often get headaches and white willow bark is more beneficial than aspirin and not so hard on the stomach.

Pau d'Arco is used a lot in South America. You can make a tea with it or get the capsules. The people who use it seem to have a much lower incidence of cancer and AIDS.

I recommend red beets to make more red blood. Meat eaters could use more liver and more red meat to help fight AIDS.

MEDICINE FOR STOMACH PROBLEMS

Slippery elm bark is very healing, because it can stay in the stomach when nothing else will. But I prefer aloe vera gel, which is also strong against most poisons or infection, and protects your stomach while you're taking other medicine. I've known it to cure cancers, ulcers, and many stomach problems. You can also use it for external burns with good results. When I had ulcers after having too many x-rays, I cured them in three days with aloe vera gel. I'd take a big spoonful three or four times a day before meals and at bedtime. Stomach ulcers are like a burn: a gas in the stomach causes the burn that causes the ulcer, and so you're doctoring the burn. Everybody nowadays seems to know that aloe vera is good for doctoring burns. Then you have to look into what causes the ulcers in the first place.

The tea described here is good for relieving a stomach ache.

1/2 cup dried peppermint
1/2 cup dried chamomile flowers
6 cups pure water

Bring water to a boil in a stainless steel pot. Reduce heat to simmer, and add herbs. Steep/simmer 15 minutes. Strain, bottle, and refrigerate. Drink 1 cup warm as needed.

MEDICINE FOR GALLSTONES

Sometimes a person is under stress and then it creates gallstones. Also, if you've been eating modern food, at some point in your life you will have gallstones. Modern medical people say one out of four people has gallstones. I say the number is higher. Many people carrying gallstones don't know until the stones back up in there and become very large.

I've got three or four jars of them at home in the refrigerator that I took out of different people. They're all colors and pretty. I'm saving them to make a necklace for my wife, but I think she threw something at me one time when I mentioned it. Women are funny you know. Sometimes they don't appreciate the things men will do for them.

Certain herbs help to pass the stones out if they haven't gone too far. The first remedy is to get away from the crappy food that modern people seem to love.

Liver and gall bladder flush

1. Take ordinary meals Monday through Saturday noon. Drink all the natural apple juice you can.
2. Two or three hours after a normal lunch on Saturday, take 2 teaspoons epsom salts or castor oil in 1 ounce of hot water.
3. For Saturday dinner drink grapefruit and orange juice or other citrus juice.
4. At bedtime on Saturday, take ½ cup cold or warm unrefined olive oil and ½ cup of either grapefruit juice or lemon juice. Go to bed immediately. Lie on your right side with knees pulled up to chest for 30 minutes.
5. On Sunday morning one hour before breakfast, take 2 teaspoons disodium phosphate or epsom salt or castor oil dissolved in 2 ounces of hot water.
6. Return to normal meals. Watch stools for green gelatinous, or dark, grape seed-size stones. If you see a large number of stones, repeat the flush at two-week intervals until stones disappear.

MEDICINE FOR WOMEN

In the Sixties, some quack put it out that women shouldn't take douches. I'd like to choke that person. I knew some young women who got to the point they were carrying so much venereal disease they couldn't have children.

Indian women have always been clean. Venereal diseases were brought from Europe first, and now there are other particularly vicious kinds from Asia. Indian women originally made douche bags out of bladders, sometimes with a smooth bone attached, and sometimes they used gourds.

Some women were told by doctors that douches wash out the natural bacteria, and they'd ask me about it. Sure they wash out some of the natural bacteria, but they also wash out a large amount of the harmful bacteria and the natural bacteria replaces itself. So using douches is good. Don't let anybody else tell you something different. Sexually transmitted diseases are a national epidemic, and it's getting worse all the time. It's gotten to the point that some women think it's normal to have some kind of discharge.

For a "high douche," lie down in the bathtub and elevate the hips where the douche water goes all the way up inside. For these douches, add a small amount of a mild liquid soap to the water. Test the water first so that you don't burn yourself. Pregnant women should not douche after the thirty-eighth week from conception, or after the cervix opens. A sage douche is good for yeast infections, and a vinegar douche is good for cleanliness.

OVARIAN/UTERINE CANCER DOUCHES

Use the hydrogen peroxide douche two times a day for two days. Then use the chaparral douche. Use the "high douche" position and hold the medicine in for 10 to 15 minutes. Pray over the medicine to give it direction and tell it what to do. Do not drink coffee or smoke cigarettes, and drink yellow dock root tea.

Hydrogen peroxide douche

½ part hydrogen peroxide
½ part sterile water

Chaparral douche

⅓ part organic iodine

⅓ part sterile water

⅓ part chaparral tea

1 tablespoon powdered alum per gallon of water

MEDICINE FOR VENEREAL DISEASE

Tea

½ pound white oak bark

2 pints apple cider vinegar

1 quart chaparral tea

1 handful dried peppermint leaves

1 handful juniper berries

Put all ingredients in a 3-gallon pot. Fill with 2 gallons of pure water. Boil 2 to 3 hours until a rich, golden color. Take ¼ cup frequently throughout the day. Also use as a douche.

Douche

Fill douche bag two-thirds full with tea. Add one large squirt of povidine iodine. Take a "high douche" twice a day until cured.

MEDICINE FOR HERPES

This tea is good for both men and women. It should be taken cold four times a day 30 minutes before mealtimes and before bed. Women should also take a "high douche" using a small amount of a liquid disinfectant, such as Hexol (manufactured by Hexol, Inc., San Francisco, California), and a small amount of mild soap, such as Green Soap (a brand-name liquid soap) or Pine Tar Soap (a brand-name bar soap).

Tea

Cut burdock root
Wild lettuce leaves
Peach leaves
Yellow dock root
Eucalyptus leaves

Boil water in a one-gallon stainless steel pot. Remove from heat and add herbs. Let steep for 30 minutes. Strain and drink. Place remainder in refrigerator.

MEDICINE FOR DEPRESSION

Something about this civilization is causing people to go crazy, and it's recorded in newspapers and magazines. Many of my psychiatrist friends tell me the same thing: that more and more people are going crazy. They tell me they do a big business nowadays and there's not enough doctors to go around. Why? Well, there are many reasons. The main ones are sugar and chemicals in food and water.

We're supposed to have pure air and pure water to cleanse our bodies and our minds. Any preservatives you take into your body, such as in food—and food is loaded with them—go to the mind, the brain. If you add more willingly to what is already there, you may go crazy.

You can be healthy eating organic food. Organically grown foods are available in stores, but sometimes the foods are not organic. Someone should periodically visit the farms where the food is grown just to make sure. Organic food might be a little more expensive, but it may be cheaper in the long run. You might want to organize your own cooperatives.

Now I know what you're thinking. How are we going to do

that and live in town? It is possible. There's still some good land out in the country, but one individual couldn't begin to go out and buy the land. Land is expensive everywhere. The only possible way is for a group of people to buy land in the country. If the people caring for the land learn the spiritual ways that go with it, you can make stuff grow anywhere.

About seventy percent of mental patients have sugar diabetes. In other words, if people allow themselves the luxury of being nasty and feeling bad, the spiritual and physical work together so they develop sugar diabetes. Such people have a great craving for sugar, and the sicker a person is the more you see them rushing out to sneak candy bars. In most cases of depression, look for sugar diabetes, an injury to the head, psychological factors from past and present lives, stress, and bad medicine. Evil spirits go right along with this unhappiness or depression.

Many young people came to our camp at Meta Tantay and got well just by being here. We told them to slow down because we find civilized people are wound up like a steel spring. The reason I mention tension and stress is that doctors have found that happy people don't get cancer as much as people who are unhappy. But what they didn't say and what is known to us is that the same thing applies to any other kind of sickness or disease. That's why a medicine man's job is not merely to wait until someone gets sick, but to conduct the right ceremonies and look after the happiness of his people, which includes whether they eat the right kinds of foods. We sing and dance and drum to drive the negative energy out, and we laugh and we joke.

Years ago I had an old doctor friend in Elko, and we'd get together every once in a while to talk about different things and have a good time. One day I asked him what he does with people who have nothing wrong with them except they can't get along with anyone, especially themselves. Such people have a negative view of everything and everyone, the whole world included. I was wondering what to do because we had a few people like that and I was getting fed up with it. Anyone can get fed up with that stuff after a while. And so the old doctor he laughed and he said, "They need to take a good shit. I give them a good laxative." So we both laughed and then I got to thinking about that, and you know, the old doctor was right. *Ho!*

Remedies

Burn incense often in your bedroom and house. Make a prayer when doing so. Also open a door or window a few inches when burning incense to give the bad energy a chance to get out.

Take tub baths and pour ½ gallon apple cider vinegar into the water.

Take a tub bath and dissolve ½ box of table salt in the tub water.

Drink 1 spoonful of apple cider vinegar 3 times a day.

Sleep with your feet toward a mountain or a body of water, or with your head toward magnetic north.

Pray often and remember that 24 hours a day is a prayer. Every thought, every action, every look is a prayer.

For job stress, get water from the ocean and pray over it so that people on your job will like you and be helpful. Take a little drink of it and wash your hands and face with it. Let the ocean water dry naturally. Your prayers will be reflected back to the people at work if spoken with kindness. Pray at home before going to work. This is only good for 24 hours.

For nervousness or insomnia steep one teaspoon ground cloves in one cup of boiling water. Steep for five minutes, and then drink.

Inhalants

1/3 pot filled with apple cider vinegar
1/3 pot filled with pure water
2 handfuls of bay leaves
1 handful of eucalyptus leaves
2 ginger roots
2 tablespoons ground cinnamon

Bring to a boil and inhale. When it cools, drink one large spoonful. Store remainder in refrigerator and use again when needed.

WARNING: *Pregnant women and people with high blood pressure should not drink the above mixture.*

Spirits of ammonia should be kept on hand at all times to be inhaled by people who have mental depression, heart trouble, lung trouble, or fainting spells.

WARNING: *Pregnant women should not inhale ammonia spirits. Next, ammonia spirits should never be taken internally by anyone.*

Citronella oil is a good inhalant. Do not use internally.

Peppermint oil is also a good safe inhalant. Put some behind your ears and at the back of the neck as well.

MEDICINE FOR COLDS, FLU, PNEUMONIA, SINUS PROBLEMS, HAY FEVER, BRONCHITIS

Take calcium, magnesium, and zinc combination tablets. Take two tablets 20 minutes before each meal and at bedtime.

Take 10,000 IUs of natural rosehip vitamin C. Take two tablets, four times a day.

Take two echinacea capsules four times a day.

Use a vaporizer with eucalyptus oil in the small reservoir. Use distilled water with ½ tablespoon of baking soda in the large reservoir.

At night rub down throat and chest with mentholatum.

Thunder Potion

This potion is ordinary and harmless, but powerful. We tried to use styrofoam cups for it once in front of a bunch of doctors, but it ate the bottom of the cups. So I had to start all over again with regular cups. But everybody swore they felt better after they tried it—even the doctors. It's good for the stomach and kidneys, opening up the head, congestion in the throat and chest, and allergies. Every person has an allergy to something. The reason is the Great Spirit wants to show us that no one is perfect. You might cure one allergy and develop another. I don't think I've ever seen this fact written in a book, but I have learned this during thirty years of medicine man medical school.

Thunder Potion is helpful for a lot of things, but it's not a cure-all. Sometimes you will need other herbal treatments for certain illnesses.

1 cup boiling water

7 drops peppermint oil

3 drops eucalyptus oil

Deeply inhale the steam from the cup. Drink when cool. Drink a cup of potion four times a day, preferably on an empty stomach.

MISCELLANEOUS MEDICINE

Tea for hepatitis/liver problems

3 gallons pure water

1 cup red sumac berries

Juice of 2 organic lemons

24 ounces red vinegar

Boil all ingredients 10 minutes. Strain, bottle, and refrigerate. Drink 2 to 4 tablespoons a day.

Tea for headache

1 cup cramp bark

1 cup white willow bark

2 quarts pure water

Boil the water, reduce heat, add the herbs, and simmer/steep for 15 to 20 minutes. Strain, bottle, and refrigerate. Drink 1 cup warm as needed.

To increase appetite

Add two droppersful of goldenseal extract to one cup of liquid. Drink twenty minutes before eating.

To improve eyesight

Add two droppersful of eyebright extract in one cup of liquid two times a day.

Remember that you should pray over all your medicine, even modern medicine, to give it strength and direction as to what you want it to do. You should pray over all your food and drink to make a healing medicine out of it.

You should also be thinking about what you're going to do with the rest of your lives; repeating the same mistakes that you've made before should not be necessary. A better life is possible for all once your own body and mind are cleaned up. There would be less pollution, less sickness, less cancer, less of the bad things of all kinds. *Ho.*

NOTES

1. Jethro Kloss, *Back to Eden* (Loma Linda, California: Back to Eden Publishing Co., 1988).

2. Chaparral was taken off the market in the United States in the late 1980s. At present chaparral is once again accessible in herb stores and elsewhere. The U.S. Food and Drug Administration does not currently have jurisdiction over herbal compounds, that is, substances labeled as "nutritional supplements."

CHAPTER SIX

Rolling Thunder, 1990.

Politics

"I'm not good material to be dictated to by any white man as to what I can do and where I can go in my own land."

Somebody told me once, "Don't make those poor white people feel bad." In our way, if something is wrong, then it's up to the medicine people to speak out. I talk pretty rough sometimes, but that's my way, and that's the way the truth has to come out. Sometimes we Indians have to raise our voices or use white people's language in order to get them to listen.

I'm not a leader of any tribe, and I never claimed to be one. I don't desire any position; I stand on my own two feet. By giving up power, I gained power—the opposite of "civilized society." I'm not here to speak for myself, but rather for all Indian people so that we can live unmolested. The American Indian would like you to understand that we've had everything taken from us. Our people are still being made war on, jailed, killed, and denied our Native foods. But we know too that there are many other bad situations in the world that should be corrected. We're interested in your welfare as well as ours because we're all brothers and sisters.

Civilized Versus Primitive

Civilized or modern people—those that stole Indian lands and polluted the world—are my enemies. I like that word "civilized" because the English language is quite tricky and misused. You have to use words that don't correctly express a true meaning.

I've been called a savage, pagan, primitive, and many other things for many years. Some of our young people looked up those words in the dictionary and it's quite interesting. "Savage" means a man who lives in the forest and close to nature. "Pagan" means "pure" in ancient Greek and "primitive" means "first" in Latin. Now what's wrong with that? I was shocked and surprised when I looked up "democracy" in the dictionary. It comes from an ancient Greek word that meant "talking out of both sides of the mouth." See how people can twist and misinterpret their own language?

Yes, I'm a savage and I can prove it. I like children. I like animals and birds, and at my age I still like women. Some of us Indians are not too civilized yet. We haven't learned to lie and steal. We don't steal other people's land and children. We don't want to make war on anybody. I haven't learned to be greedy, so I'm not civilized.

For no amount of money would I live among civilized men. At our camp we had no locks on the doors, and we'd throw out anyone who committed a crime. There's much I don't understand about civilized society, and I don't think that I ever will. I don't understand unemployment, an economic system that is falling apart, or wars. And I don't understand the breaking of the treaties.

The "wild" coyotes north of our camp kept their agreements not to bother our stock, but civilized dogs are different. You can't trust them. We had three dogs get in our rabbit pens and kill thirty rabbits. We've never had anything like that happen with the coyotes. They're not civilized so they kept their agreement with us.

We're law abiding people. According to a bulletin of the American Bar Association, the U.S. Constitution was copied almost word for word from the Iroquois Confederation. The people who wrote the Constitution didn't invent it—there was nothing like it across the Great Waters. Instead, they had the Inquisition, kings, emperors, the Dark Ages, the Thirty Years War, oppression, genocide against their own people and anyone who got in their way.

In other words, the Constitution of this country was one of the finest documents ever written, but they couldn't live by it simply because their hearts and minds were not with it then and to this day. If they could have followed the Constitution it would have been a great thing and we'd still be a great nation. We've lost our spiritual values, we're losing friends all over the world, and you can't buy friends with military dictatorships.

Buckskin Curtain

A long time ago when I first started to travel, I'd get on the stage in front of three or four thousand people, and most were white-eyes. I think the Indian was born afraid of the white man, so I'd look out there and forget what I was supposed to say, as well as the songs. I'd forget everything. But we found out later that many of those white people were afraid of us too. Now that's a terrible thing, people being afraid of each other because of wrong teachings. It's a terrible way to live because people need each other. We are trying to break down a part of that Buckskin Curtain, the white man's know-it-all attitude brought to this land.

There was an Iron Curtain in Europe and a Bamboo Curtain in the Far East. In this country, there has always been a Buckskin Curtain between the Indians and other people, and it was created by lies in history books. The white man and Indians have been at war with each other ever since the pilgrims turned on the Indians three years after their arrival in the so-called New World. Our people were scalped by the white men; scalping wasn't something we introduced.

We Indians have survived under very adverse conditions. The more they tried genocide, the more we rebelled, and we're still rebelling in a peaceful way. We do not use petitions anymore. We used to take up petitions with thousands of names on them and send them to Washington. Sometimes we'd get a two-line letter back, but usually not. When we would get an answer, it was referred back to the Bureau of Indian Affairs where it likely went in the wastebasket. Those times are gone; we work in different ways now.

We Indians have been suffering for a long time. We are under twenty-seven governments with no nation of our own. The white men made the treaties and the laws but they don't want to keep the treaties. The old ones have told me that the white men will eventually have to live by them.

Traditional and Other Indians

Two types of Indians have evolved in America. One is the white man's Indian and the other type is the traditional, or original, Indian. The red apples and uncle tommyhawks might have dark skin but they are white on the inside. They've been ed-

ucated, but it's a brainwashing kind of education so they forget the old ways and the real values. Many were brainwashed to be ashamed of being Indian, and that's a real bad feeling to have about yourself. In the old days, some Indians who scouted for the white soldiers were like this as well.

The red apples are worse than the white man. There is only one type of person worse than a crooked white man and that's any Indian who turns his back on his people. The Shoshone say that this type of Indian creates his own destruction and his trail might be short.

The white man killed our chiefs and selected puppet councils to rule over us. Many of the tribal councils were organized by the government under the Indian Reorganization Act and they do the BIA's bidding, whatever it is. The government appointed a bunch of red apples as their puppets to rule over us under the thumb of the BIA.

On the reservations rigged elections have put the white man's Indians in power. I did not work or try to work with these kinds of Indians because I disagree with most of the things they are doing. They've already sold out and now have control of all the money. The BIA continues to give money to them even when they are extremely unpopular with the people. In one election that I know of the uncle tommyhawks were so unpopular that only one man voted.

Uncle tommyhawks agree to whatever the government wants. You will see them sometimes in the BIA offices or living very comfortably while some of their own brothers and sisters, their own people, are starving to death. They're the ones who sell out Mother Earth and perpetrate other things that the masses of people do not agree with.

Because only the Great Spirit owns Mother Earth, it's impossible to sell it except by the white man's law, and we do not recognize such law. The uncle tommyhawks will sell the land for a few cents an acre and give away our oil rights and hunting rights. These arrangements are called Indian claims, and they look good for propaganda purposes. But we are forced to buy back land stolen from us. In one place Indians were paid off at thirty-seven cents an acre, while we are paying eighty-eight dollars an acre to get our own land back. This is the worst kind of deal, and the white man has pulled it from the east coast to the west coast. It will continue as long as they can do so in a court of law and as long as there are red apple Indians to sign the papers.

Some of our people do not know what they're doing—they are not educated to read papers, especially the fine print. Many Indians have become intimidated and afraid of their own councils as well as the BIA, and they are afraid to vote on council matters. Because sold-out Indians cannot represent traditionals, we have no representation. If traditionalists attempt to resist, they're ridiculed, put in jail, or worse. The government does not recognize traditional Indians and we don't recognize them or their conjured up authority.

The first puppet council in recorded history was the Jewish puppet council under the Romans, and I've been in meetings with puppet councils like that in Arizona. It's the council that tries to make it look as if the Hopis are fighting with the Navajos, but that's not true.

I am not a chief of the Shoshone and I resent it when people call me chief. In the past I have been what can be referred to as a leader, but more likely a teacher. At one time I was a spokesman among the traditional people and a spokesman for Chief Temoke of the traditional Shoshoni.

I've made myself unpopular, and I am damn proud of it. I do not want to be popular with sell-out Indians. I don't want them within arm's length of me. In the past we would all quiet down when a red apple came around. We were expected to quiet down and listen to the educated ones who turned traitor, who the government put in office to represent the Indians, but those days are gone. Some of us hang on to traditional Indian ways and there are masses of people who have no use for the puppet councils. I have never sold out, so I'm a traditional Indian. Some uncle tommyhawk Indians don't like me, and you know what I tell them? I tell them they can go along with the white man to the same place.

Determining whether to be a puppet is up to the person him or herself. I am not the judge or policeman. I also refuse to consider one tribe as being superior to another, or even that we are superior to some white people, as long as they do not lie or steal, or go along with the lying or stealing.

Some Indian people have lost proper respect for each other; they talk bad about each other and create rumors. This cuts us down just as much as alcohol, so we have to get over it. We Indians are not sitting around these days blaming the white people for all of our problems, but we're not making excuses either for anybody that's got it coming, like those who steal our children.

Dimensions of Genocide

The white man never gave us anything good. We gave them our best foods, our best medicines. We gave up our land, our children. The only thing they couldn't steal was our souls, unless an Indian was so dumb as to give it up himself. But they tried that too.

The genocide program against the American Indian is still ongoing. You may not be ready to hear about these things. I know there are many good people who are not aware of genocide, just like the German people. I asked some Germans about Auschwitz and genocide against the Jewish people, and they said they didn't know what was going on. I then asked them if they really wanted to know. To the American people I ask if they want to know the truth about genocide, such as the sterilization of Indian women.

The proof is there for anybody who really wants to look into it. By "civilized" society's own statistics, fifty-five percent of the women of childbearing age of the Crow tribe in Montana have been sterilized. Most were sterilized without their knowledge or consent. Such sterilization programs are still going on all over the country.

Now that's pretty damn gruesome, and yet politicians and others want to talk about what the Nazis did in Germany or what the Russians are doing. To them the same things taking place here are somehow different. I do not listen to them when they say that we are better off than other people somewhere else. Well, maybe so and maybe not, but let's clean up our own house first. The thing they wished for, the vanishing Indian, did not happen. Our numbers are now growing faster than any other group in proportion to the population. About sixty years ago, something happened and it happened almost overnight. The medicine people knew what it was all about. The disappearance of the Indians was not meant to happen, so things reversed themselves. But they have not given up, so they are trying to bring about genocide by sterilizing Indian women.

I know the reputations of some big corporations too. Ma

Bell together with the CIA helped overthrow the only president whoever did one damn thing for the Indians and that was President Salvador Allende some years ago in Chile. He returned land to many Indians and peasants. But Ma Bell and the CIA went in there and killed that man in the presidential palace. The first ones the soldiers then went after were the Indians. They said the Indians were communists. Hell, the Indians didn't even know what a communist was. But when they get a lot of publicity they can make a communist out of whoever they want to, and I guess they did. By now they've killed an awful lot of people. A few Indians escaped over the Andes Mountains to Argentina.

For money they prop up dictatorships like in Guatemala, El Salvador, and Nicaragua, and other places where they are killing our people. Thousands of Mayans in Guatemala and across the border in Mexico have been killed or removed from their land: this is genocide.

A few years ago someone took pictures of a ship standing off San Francisco spraying the town with a deadly kind of sickness. A few died but no one had any proof except for the pictures of one man who died. Our government would never do such a thing, right? Well, the government does use germ warfare. They've been using it on us Indians for many years. Examples are blankets loaded with smallpox germs, and planting rabies on a part of the Navajo reservation when they decided there were too many Navajos and their numbers were growing too fast.

After much research and diabolical testing, they are very experienced. Now they can continue their genocide program against American Indians using the Hanta virus, the so-called mystery disease. It started in the Four Corners area near the

Navajo reservation, at a place where they had to shut down an experimental place because of military budget cuts. They took those rats they'd been experimenting on and turned them loose. They promptly mixed with the local rats and mice and then the ground squirrels. The disease itself travels mostly through the fecal matter of animals as well as humans.

This mystery disease is similar to other diseases that cause difficulty in getting one's breath, and the lungs fill with water. It cripples and then paralyzes people. We can't accuse anyone at this time because it's hard to prove, but it is a fact that the disease affects Indian and Mexican people a lot worse than it does the whites. It only kills whites once in a while. The hot spots are localized, and the biggest one of all is on the Navajo reservation. The whites call it a flu because it doesn't affect them nearly as bad as it does Indians.

We have to find ways of countering this sickness. We Native people are going to have to find our own remedies just like we have in the past, and not wait for the chemical companies and the government and health care services to provide a cure. I have a number of friends who are doctors or connected with the CIA who have been doing research and gathering information on this. That's part of my work too.

THE LAND

We are under twenty-seven governments with no nation of our own. The white man's government made the treaties and the laws, but they don't want to keep the treaties. An example is that Chief Justice John Marshall ruled that the Cherokee were a sovereign nation. But, the president of the United States, Andrew Jackson, chose to ignore this law. Soldiers invaded

Cherokee country and sent many into exile a thousand miles to the west on a death march.

Then by an act of Congress in 1924 Indians were made citizens of the United States by force. They call us citizens but we were not asked. They made us citizens mostly so that they could tax and draft us. We cannot understand why we should pay taxes to gather piñon nuts and graze horses on our own land. We can't understand why we should pay taxes to hunt the deer that belong to us. Many of our people up in the northwest can't fish. They have to slip out at night to fish in order to feed their families. They are denying us a livelihood and it amounts to economic genocide.

In the Treaty of Ruby Valley the Shoshone didn't give up any land. The treaty gave the white settlers the right to pass through and to establish industries of their own. But the whites have declared war on us and they're in violation of the treaty. They passed some new laws and now the Bureau of Land Management says we should pay taxes and grazing fees. The reservations here are small and so the Indians living on the reservations don't have range rights. Off the reservation they cannot operate as an economic unit and can't compete with the big ranchers who can and will pay taxes.

In Oklahoma I have seen many Indians arbitrarily deprived of their land by being put on the tax rolls without their knowledge or permission. In Nevada I have seen a map of Indian lands all over Ruby Valley and yet no Indian can live on those lands. They are leased to white men, but who gets the money? Nobody knows.

We should not be treated as if we are somebody's cattle, like those ten thousand Navajos and a number of Hopis they're moving out of their homes and off their land so that the

Peabody Coal Company in Arizona can mine the coal and drill for oil and uranium. Before Peabody, no one bothered the Indians in that area. Now this big coal company is like a monster after the minerals and they've made those Navajos helpless. The first thing they did was take away their sheep and goats. The Navajos were placed in an area where they can't make a living, and they even have to haul water for miles because the government never considered drilling wells for them. They end up moving to Flagstaff and other cities, living in some clapboard government kind of housing in an area where there's no livelihood, no jobs, and they become complete refugees.

The loss of land has been so terrific that millions of Indians in the United States and Canada have no home whatsoever in our own country. We have been continually told that according to the white man's law, the land belongs to the Indians and is held in trust for the Indians to be protected from loss and exploitation. But crooked lawyers are hired by the government to represent the Indian people in claims against the government. These lawyers become millionaires as the Indians get poorer and more landless.

When James Watt was Secretary of the Interior he insulted the Indian people. He dwelt on the fact that there is much more alcoholism, drug abuse, and other bad things among our Indian people. You find the same thing among any conquered people anywhere when they have nothing else to do and no hope for the future, where everything, including most of the land, was stolen from them. We knew that Watt's words were only a ploy to steal more Indian land. And I think a lot of other people saw through it too, that it was the same old trick to try to separate us from Mother Earth to make us extinct. I was proud to be an Indian then because all Indians protested, even those we refer to as uncle tommyhawks. So Watt did one good thing, if nothing else: he really woke our people up.

CULTURAL ANNIHILATION

The government has tried to make all Indians over in the white man's image—in language, religion, and education. All Indians were forced to adopt white names, and there were no exceptions. Since the early days we had to adopt white names to be enrolled in school or to hold a job. The general public doesn't know that Indian people were forced by the government to take white names. It's not our choice to be called by a foreign name.

Our pride has been taken away. That's why our people sank to a low point of drinking, suicide, and many other bad things. From the first time the Europeans set foot on this land they took our children to be brainwashed in their schools. Education was left up to the missionaries, who were mostly fanatical Christians who called Indians heathens and other bad names. Much of the value of our culture has been lost because for many years we were told it was no good to learn these things. For many years our young people did not keep up with the culture; it's a shame because we have a complex culture that came from this land, and there is no other that can fit this land or replace it.

The Indian agents used to come and haul the Indian kids off to school. The Indian schools were awful, and many of the kids would walk all the way home and hide out from the authorities. My folks sent me to white schools so that I wouldn't be brainwashed in reservation schools. They wanted me to get a good education so that someday I could talk for my people. I went to the first year of high school and then dropped out. Although I believed that my education was better than the brainwashing in reservation schools, I began to suspect that many of the old people who didn't speak English had more knowledge in some ways than a lot of the people who were "educated." The real knowledge wasn't in the schools.

White people still go to the reservations and kidnap children and give them to the Mormons under the guise of providing them with a good home and an education. People should not have to live in fear like the Indians do to this day. They do not know when someone may come and take their children away to distant boarding schools or adopt them out to white families. Many Indians willingly gave up their children because they could not feed them, but there are cases where uncles or grandparents or the tribe would have taken the children in. Instead, they were adopted out to white people because when the law favors Indians, suddenly it's twisted and made to help the white man.

In many cases, Indian children are adopted out to white families so that those families have a little servant for free while the child grows up. We checked on one girl who was kidnapped or farmed out like that. She had one suit of clothes and whip marks way up to her behind. She didn't do the housework when the old biddy went to socials. When the biddy came home and the housework was not done, the girl got a beating.

Children removed from the reservations are made ashamed to be Indians, and become more confused. They know nothing about their people's way of life. Many of them are full-bloods, and cannot speak one word of their own language. Many are forbidden to speak their language, and they become afraid of their own people. These Indian young people are taught to be helpless in their own society, and to take the most menial jobs in the white man's society when they have to relocate to the cities.

When these children get old enough to escape there are only two alternatives to them: to integrate into "civilized" society, and they're never happy that way, or to become drinkers or militants because they've been hurt. I knew of one young Indian at our camp who had been a hero at Wounded Knee. The government told the Indians after the surrender that they could go home. Instead, men, women, and children were beaten. This young man had ridges in his head where they had beat him, with blood and pus still oozing out of his scalp. He told me the story of how he was adopted out when he was young. He was one of the lucky ones who happened to know who his relations were. But when his own mother died, his foster family wouldn't let him go to her funeral, and he was very bitter. He'll always be a militant; he's ruined for life. Many of our young people have been ruined instead of being taught about love and how to relate to nature and to Great Spirit.

There are thousands of young Indians who have been raised away from their people. I've met many who never knew their parents or their own people. They have lost their trail. But when they come into contact with traditionals and once they know a few of the Great Spirit's teachings and the law of this land, they give up the bottle and other bad things. And they know they don't have to be ashamed of who they are.

IMPRISONMENT

There are relatively few traditional families left, and there is no traditional family without someone missing, dead, or in prison. Before Wounded Knee we had three times the number (proportionately) of any other ethnic group in prison. Since Wounded Knee there are many more.

We have a great many political prisoners in jail at this time, including Leonard Peltier, who fought at Wounded Knee. He was a hero. He would slip out at night into the trenches of the federals and steal their food and take it back to the women and children. He was a big man but he didn't eat. He fasted for days. Leonard did not do what the government accused him of, but he wouldn't tell them who did.

When Leonard was held in a prison close to Vancouver, Canada, at a big meeting and ceremony I was delegated to go into the prison. I was invited to go in and see him and do what needed to be done; all I needed was an invitation, because I don't go anywhere unless I'm invited. At the time his own lawyer and his family couldn't get in to see him. I went with a big convoy of Indians, and in the parking lot I told them I would go in by myself. I took everything out that I had in my pockets—my identification, my wallet, and so on. The only things I took in with me were my eagle feather, and one for Leonard. I also took something else so that they wouldn't kill him.

When I got to the front gate it was open and the guard was looking the other way. So I thought, well, that's for me, so I just walked on in. Of course, I had to go through five or six of those big iron gates with a guard at every one of them. That was the toughest prison I've ever been in; tougher even than Leavenworth. Nobody ever smiled, and I walked by a lot of guards, administrators, and wardens. But I'd just stand there a few minutes holding my eagle feather and look at the guard and then he'd come down and unlock the gate. I passed through with no problem whatsoever right into the central part.

When I got to the central part the gates were closed and locked, and right behind them was a guard standing like a robot at attention with a rifle over his shoulder and a pistol on his hip. But he came down, unlocked the gate and stood back. I went on to where they had Leonard. He was in something like an animal cage with bars all the way around, and his wrists and his legs were shackled together. I went inside the cage with him and talked to him quietly a few minutes. I explained things to him in a way so that they wouldn't hang him like they planned to do when they got him back to the United States. It was absolutely necessary because all the Indians knew, everyone knew, what they were going to do if they got him back to South Dakota. Then I came back out with no problems.

The trail had been cleared: Leonard's attorney and his family came through a little later. We also had a big demonstration for him in one of those big public squares in Vancouver. Indians from all over and thousands of other people joined in, and it went off peacefully with no violence whatsoever. There were seven eagles that came down and circled as the demonstration was going on. There was a lot of power at work there.

So anyway, Leonard's still alive. He got two life sentences after they extradited him, but they didn't kill him. So the mission was successful and he'll never serve all that sentence. Leonard certainly is a hero, and no one can say he is not. We have many political and war prisoners in jail. It's the white people who did this to Leonard and it's the white people who are getting themselves in the most trouble nowadays.

I think they made a big mistake in not releasing Leonard. Billions of dollars could be saved by simply letting this man go. When President Clinton was in San Francisco to celebrate the formation of the United Nations fifty years ago, he was not available to sign the executive clemency for Leonard. Afterward, it started to rain and flood in Washington, D.C. This matter has been turned over to the Great Spirit, and there have been many high winds and floods.

INTIMIDATION AND MISINFORMATION

Any of us—medicine men, chiefs—who travel these days always have people around to watch out for us. The reason why some of us are still around is only by the power of the Great Spirit. I have been shot at, and they have tried to poison me many times. I have had guards around my house at certain times, especially during Wounded Knee. We've even had FBI and CIA agents stay in our camp (Meta Tantay). We didn't care because we had nothing to hide. We knew who they were all the time.

My enemies in high places tell me that I might go anytime, that it's the short trail for me. I've been warned many times not to speak to groups of people, that it could be dangerous. But there's only one time to die. When my time comes, at least I'll go without a guilty conscience. Don't ever listen to anybody who says I committed suicide.

We were visited when we first established our camp by some racist people who came at night. But we knew they were coming so I had about fifteen young warriors there to give them a proper reception. When we got through with them out there in the dark, they never came again at night or in that kind of way. I didn't let the warriors use knives or guns or anything like that because we really don't like to hurt people. You'd hear a thump and a yelp every once in a while, but they were intentionally allowed to get away.

I was speaking in California the day before Mount Saint Helens blew up. I told a big audience about the volcanoes that were going to erupt. When I got home I got a call from a CIA man, and he told me the government is not letting people know about the volcanoes and other harm across the country that is on the way. I said, "Yes, but I am." It's the same old thing. He continually warns me and my friends warn me, "Don't knock the politicians and the government, whatever you do."

We have tried getting the message to the United Nations, including at the Spiritual Unity Conference in 1975. In meetings with the medicine people, it was decided that Grandfather David Monongye, a Hopi elder and keeper of the prophecies, should go and deliver a message. We knew this man was the one whose prophecies told him many years ago that he was to deliver the message to the House of Mica. The prophecy, which preceded both the Mayflower and Columbus, stated that the House of Mica would be built on the waters to the east.

I went to New York City in 1975 with others to accompany Grandfather Monongye—who was over one hundred years old at the time—to see that he got there safely. They threatened to assassinate me at the gate; they were mad at all of us and me in particular for some reason I didn't understand. The CIA, the FBI, any of the other outfits could get me anytime they wanted, but I knew they wouldn't have the guts to do it there. It would be kind of messy, bad publicity. So we got into the United Nations all right.

I went right on in with Grandfather David; I held an eagle feather behind his head and another young Indian laid his hand on Grandfather David's shoulder for eight hours so that he wouldn't get tired and go to sleep. But David Monongye was never called on to speak. He wasn't allowed to speak.

The prophecy indicated that there would be a spiritual meeting of the great religions of the world in the House of Mica, where all nations would meet to try to achieve peace. There were lots of politicians, representatives, and religious leaders of the world; the Jews, the Catholics, the Moslems, the Christians, and the Buddhists. All of them got to talk, and they talked very nicely and presented some good ideas, but the little bit to be added by the American Indians and the Tibetan people was never spoken. That little bit may have brought about world peace. After being invited, no American Indian was allowed to speak, nor were the Tibetans. All the others spoke, and I give them credit because they were all on a high level. But they didn't want to hear the little bit to be added to bring about the peace for the brotherhood of man. They weren't ready to hear it.

They had a CIA man running the meeting with a pistol on his hip under his coat. They ran out of time when it came time for the Tibetans and the Indians to speak. We found out later that there were several major governments, the lefts and the rights, who did not want the original peoples to speak. So they conveniently ran out of time.

They sent for us the next day; they suddenly decided that Grandfather Monongye's statement might be important, and they would hear it in private. We turned them down. We told them that they had missed the chance. We came to understand that they didn't really want peace, so that's where it stands. The warnings have been delivered, and the job was done. Those people had their own thing going. The different governments had already made up their minds, so they weren't about to listen to us Indians. They're still going ahead and preparing for the next world war. They missed the boat, just like they've been missing the boat ever since they've been here.

People should consider visiting with the Indians themselves to learn what is going on instead of listening to the lies,
such as about Wounded Knee, where they tried to make out
the Indians as the aggressors. In all the news coverage, only one
side was told, not ours. Yet, they were on Indian land, shooting at the Indians. There were even lots of foreign journalists
at Wounded Knee, but everything was censored. It was all lies.

LIFE ON THE RESERVATION

Many Indians nowadays live off the reservations because they
keep stealing the land and there's not enough room. Besides,
on the reservations Indians can do very little unless they are
sell-out Indians. We have a dictator, the Indian agent, breathing down our necks. He can shut off the water that we use to
irrigate if we protest something. We live under a dictatorship
of the worst kind.

It's a different world out there on the reservations where
the Indian agent is the law. There's more than eighty percent
unemployment when times are good, with many of the people
forced to limit themselves to one meal a day. It's shameful that
we have to sneak out at night to hunt and fish to feed our families. In this country there's a scarcity of fish and deer, but they
are reserved for the sportsmen who can pay their taxes. Then
they want to blame the Indians for what small amounts we take
for food.

People usually think the Indian agents are there to protect
the rights and property of the Indian people, but that has never
been the case. Most Indians have a good sense of humor. We
like to laugh or joke until we see a missionary or an Indian
agent coming. Then we won't say a word because those people

are all on the make. They walk up to us and everybody suddenly forgets they can speak English. We had our camp, Meta Tantay, off the reservation where we could do as we damn well pleased. No commissar Indian agent looked down our collar or shut off our irrigation water if we didn't look right or do right. There are three classes of people we don't allow on land we control: politicians, Indian agents, and missionaries.

The Indian agent is a commissar who can annul any act of the puppet tribal council, especially if the council tries to do something useful for the people. Not all councils are puppets. Some of them try to help their people, but they are allowed to go only so far. There have been times when the puppet council itself forgets to do the bidding of the Bureau of Indian Affairs. When this happens the government goes to great extremes to discredit Indians who stand up for their rights. Thus, the beauty of Indian life is gone on the reservation.

I'm not opposed to the law—some of the police are okay. The police are supposed to enforce law and order for all people, including minorities and poor people. People are often in fear for their lives on the reservation. The good people fear the agency police.

DESECRATION OF GRAVES

A long time ago it was prophesied that a day would come when we would have to draw a line that white people cannot go beyond. That line has been drawn. We don't want our graves disturbed. People dig in our graves and give themselves long names such as "anthropologist," instead of asking us what they want to know. We will never dig for other people's bones because it's an amateurish, ghoulish way of going about getting information—it's not necessary, it's wrong, it's desecration! We see the damn fools going out there and digging in an Indian grave because they have no respect. The white man has a fetish at this time for Indian skeletons in their museums.

On the little reservation in Ruby Valley we caught two people digging in Indian graves. I wanted the Indians to wait until I could get some photographers, newspaper people, and maybe some law enforcement types that might be interested in coming out to record it. Well, the Indians didn't wait. They told those guys to fill up that hole, and that the next time they'd put them in that hole.

I talked to an anthropology class once in Alaska, and I didn't tell them what they wanted to hear. I think I really shook some of them up when I told them they were doing wrong. I told those people the truth, as well as what their own karma is going to be. Two or three were showing it already. They were sitting there shaking, starting to become paralyzed on one side with one eye rolling up in the head and one eye batting. That's a sure sign they had been digging in Indian graves. They're going to pay for it until they get wise and overcome some of their foolishness.

The Louisiana flood in 1983 took place because anthropologists disturbed sacred Indian grave mounds. I was there and I warned them, but they wouldn't listen. As soon as I left, the great flood came. I saw it on television and in the papers; it was the biggest flood they ever had.

Indian Resistance

Years ago people used to talk about the "vanishing Indian." There was even a picture they used to hang on the wall with an

Indian and his horse, both of their heads hanging down, riding into the sunset. Well, I hated that damn thing even when I was a kid. I found out later that every other Indian also hated that picture. You don't see it much anymore, and there's a reason for it. My people are not a vanishing breed, they are alive and increasing, and we're coming back real fast. We will have that better life, one way or another. We will learn to live together or no one will live here at all.

I used to be scared to death every time I had to talk to an Indian agent or politician. People thought I was afraid of nothing, but my heart would beat like a drum when I would face Mr. Whiteman sitting behind a desk, and he'd look like he could eat us all up and spit us out. It took me a long time; I had to go through a lot of ceremonies, do a lot of praying and listening to the drum before I finally found out it wasn't true. That white man, whoever he is, doesn't have all the power because no one has all the power. That power belongs to Great Spirit, the Creator.

After a while, I began to understand that we'd been lied to. We'd become brainwashed as children and it took me a long time to figure out that they're just people like anybody else, not better, and certainly not worse. So that's the way it is today. We turn our backs on the things they brought here—the alcohol, the dope, the phony lying laws where they promise one thing and give us another or nothing at all. Once we turn our backs on these things and put our faith where it belongs, nothing is going to keep us down anymore.

The pride and the spirit are back again with the people. Many of our people are turning back to the Great Spirit's power, the only sovereign we've ever recognized. Our people are getting stronger within themselves. They can stand up now and have no excuse for trying to pretend to be anything else than what we were intended to be. We are quite independent and that's the way we're supposed to be. We like to see our people able to stand on their own feet and proudly walk anywhere. I suppose that this is why some people in the government say they have never been able to do anything with the Indians. I don't know who told them they were supposed to do something with us—I have yet to figure that out.

It is true that they have never been able to do anything with the Indian because we make poor material for any kind of serf or slave. We know that all people know best how they want to live. We don't need foreigners to come here and tell us how to do it. We are a free people and happy after suffering much. Even though we are under a lot of stress and in some places under the gun, please do not be sorry for us Indians because the spirit power is back and we're with it.

I did my job on the Billy Jack movies of directing the Indian parts, as well as seeing to it that we had clear weather. It did stay clear during the entire filming. I think those movies carried a message based on the realism of things happening on the reservations that the public was totally unaware of, and that somebody is doing something about it.

We see our families and our tribes coming back together again, cleaning themselves up, wearing their hair long, and wearing the red headbands. More and more Indians are returning to their heritage. That's what it was at Wounded Knee—every person, every young person there was a hero. These young people were on their own land and resisting in a token way, but they showed that we are still men. Nowadays we can stand up and speak out that we are not aggressive, that we are a strong people. We find that in just about every case when an Indian gets older, he'll go back to the blanket. I love it. We're always glad to take him back.

I've been called a militant. Yes, I'm a militant. So was the great healer, the one called Jesus Christ. I'm a militant even if I no longer carry a gun. We are warriors fighting for peace. I'm not here to advocate violence, but anyone will defend themselves or their families. Our people are not ordinarily rude unless someone is rude to us.

No matter how tough another person is, how much of a Nazi or a puritan, or how much of a witch, or how mean, I'll still try three times to get a good relationship going. But on that third try I'd better get a good thought back, a good vibe, a good intention, because I'm not a Christian and I don't do good for evil. We do good for good. Let's be honest. Nobody else does good for evil either. Nobody else turns the other cheek. How are you gonna thank someone if they force aggression on you? When they come into your country and your home and make war on you after you have peace treaties? And after they gave their word, not in surrender but in treaties of peace and friendship? How are you going to thank someone like that? How would anyone like it if foreign soldiers came here to steal children or sterilize women?

Being peaceful does not mean that we can be pushed around. We think we can take care of ourselves very well as long as no one uses violence or molests us. But if it came down to that, we're not afraid to die because we don't have a guilty conscience.

But at this time we no longer can fight. To tell you the truth, if we could, I'd be worse than Geronimo. We're warriors and we're men. We could fight if we had to, but we're less than a half of one percent of the population. Anyway, there is no permanent victory for anyone in military action. My father fought and I'm proud of it. I've been there too in different places and different countries. There's no permanent victory; that's what I had to learn.

I've been involved in little contests where martial arts and sometimes old guns would be used. There was no law enforced for the benefit of Indians in those days, and we had to do the best we could with what we had. But in all the raids that I've been involved in, no one was ever shot. We had perfect discipline; besides, our men and women warriors were doctored in such a way that the enemy actually dropped their guns. Everything was efficient and went like clockwork so that not even the law enforcement people could complain.

We want to put the wars away from us. We're not supposed to be involved. Every time in the past when we've fought on one side or the other, it turned out to be the wrong side, like when the Iroquois fought on the side of George Washington against the French. They lost some land immediately, and the soldiers turned on them. Our prophecies tell us not to take sides.

Fighting with each other and aggression, these things of the past, really have to stop. Do we have to prove to the white man that Indians are necessary? That colonialism is dead not only in Russia, but right here too? That there never was a super race? Colonialism and super race concepts have to go by the wayside, as they make for war not peace. People must learn to recognize each other so that peace can be possible. In many places where I have been there are redneck and Nazi American elements. If I don't see six or seven people get up and walk out at the first part of my talk, then I figure my talk has had no meaning and no success. Once they leave the air is cleared and the people come together as one and the understanding comes to us all.

I would like to see more protests in peaceful ways. I don't think violence is the answer now. That's what we are trying to get away from. You can be a gentleman or a lady and still be a militant. You don't have to rebel against everything, but against anything evil. There's a lot of cleaning up to do. Where do you start? It has to start within yourself and violence has no place. What good is a bow and arrow or even a gun against an atomic bomb, anyway? None at all. Nowadays the older ones among our people are telling all our people and others to put the guns away, put the violence aside, and to put their hearts and minds together and learn to walk with the truth.

We do not hold grudges. We like to have friends and brothers but not of the colonial mind-set. Some people actually believe that because they belong to a particular race that they should rule the world. Well, other people have tried that and failed. Oh, they would bring death to a lot of people all right, but every one of them failed in the end, and this country is going to fail as well because it isn't meant to be.

Among my people it is said that one man is not supposed to tell another what to do. In other words, we are not made to be told by anyone else what we can and cannot do. White people would be better off if they could get with it and realize that one fact of life. Indians are not here merely for their benefit. I say it's time for all people to get over their hangups. Our prophecies tell us that the way of life of civilized society is going down, but it doesn't have to be that way.

Regarding hate for anyone or white people, that's not Indian and never was. A little kindness and the Indians just naturally come around real fast. We have turned it over to the

Great Spirit. We don't wish bad luck on anyone, but there is such a thing as karma. If peace is not made with the American Indians, nobody will have any influence on the weather and there will be chaos in the streets. If you can't get along with us First People, you certainly can't get along with other people.

We Indians, the Native people, are the last ones who don't want this land destroyed because we are the keepers of this land. There's more power in our medicine, good medicine, than there is in everything non-Indian society has. There's more power in one lightning bolt than in the first atomic bomb they dropped on Japan. I think that was proved when four prongs of lightning hit different powerhouses and blacked out New York City. One of them hit a place called Indian Point. Quite a coincidence, huh? We've got people who can bring down the lightning at any place at any time. It's said that four of our spiritual warriors would be able to destroy a great city with no weapons in their hands.[1] There's more power in an eagle feather than in a man's fist. So it's not like we're a defenseless people. But the more power you have, the more careful you have to be. Maybe governments don't agree with this, but I do.

The elements and the animals are on our side. Whether or not you can prove it in scientific laboratories, I don't know. But while you're trying to prove it, it's already happening. And it might be too late by the time you get around to proving it and writing a book about it.

For example, we found water at seven feet on our land in the desert where others couldn't find it, because the Great Spirit wanted us to have it. Back in 1992, the Bureau of Land Management was rounding up Shoshone cattle with helicopters and chasing the Indians across the desert with one of those helicopters. I think it was the day before Thanksgiving. One of the biggest blizzards recorded in one hundred years came and downed the helicopters because the pilots couldn't see where they were going. The blizzard stopped the big trucks that were hauling out the Shoshone cattle and horses. Of course, I'm not superstitious, it was just a coincidence. But I think the Grandfather heard our drums going and our prayers at that time.

ON FREEDOM

Lots of people talk about freedom and they don't know the first meaning of the word. We have a long history of fighting for our freedom when we had to. When we're talking about freedom we're not talking about politics as usual in this country. We're talking about the right to live, and that means the right to live our own lives. When we sing and talk about freedom we're not merely thinking of ourselves. We also think of other people around the world.

There are different ways of being free. Freedom can be freedom from fear, freedom from hunger, freedom from sickness, freedom from bad thoughts. There are really many ways of being a free people and it's a good feeling.

We Indians are free people today. We never forgot how to be free, and we have never accepted dictatorship. We live under twenty-seven different foreign governments and yet we still consider ourselves free. Our treaties are based on friendship and peace—never surrender. No Indian ever really surrendered. Maybe that's why they killed so many millions of us in all those twenty-seven governments in North, Central, and

South America. Maybe that's why they're still doing it. We have to contend with the Bureau of Indian Affairs, Federal Bureau of Investigation, Central Intelligence Agency, and others because we recognize no dictator of any kind from wherever they might come from. We recognize only one sovereign, the Great Spirit.

Atonement

I talk to people, try to get them to listen, to get off their asses and working for a solution. It's not us who break the treaties and lie and then become sick. Modern people don't seem to understand that they bring this on themselves. Everything can be changed to the better for everyone.

White society is going to have one more chance and that'll be the third time, the last opportunity to make atonement and right the wrongs. I don't think I'll tell you about that chance at this time because I am not supposed to enter into white people's politics. We can only tell so much of what we know; we like people to think for themselves. But I will tell you that there is still hope. Unless people come together in the right ways to remedy wrongs committed on this land and against the First People, things will get very rough. There isn't much time.

White people will have to find a white man because it's their government. I admit that I've never voted in my life because I don't interfere in other people's business. I am not qualified to help them select their chiefs, but I'm not telling you that you shouldn't vote. This man will have the law and the power, and anytime he wants to he can do good. He can stop the bad things being done against the land and the First People. There is such a person. The non-Indians will have to find him and put him in office, but they haven't got long to do it. He will not only have to be a strong man, he'll have to be a type of spiritual warrior. He'll have to have a high spiritual power, because if not, they will assassinate him. Some people have asked me where they can find him. That's not my business but we are still waiting for him.

He's going to have to consider the fact that people need help instead of spending money on atomic bombs, propping up every dictatorship on the face of the earth, and trying to buy friends. It's hard to tell nowadays who's going to represent the people. I'm looking for a politician who will keep the treaties. Then I'll know I've met an honest man and we can sit down and make peace and live in peace.

I used to meet with politicians all the time, but we don't do it anymore. I made an exception with Governor Jerry Brown of California, as I met with him once. I believe he was sincere, and I have noticed that he seems to be a pretty good man. At least he didn't allow them to extradite Dennis Banks back to South Dakota, where they wanted to kill him. Governor Brown refused to sign the extradition, and he did so against major opposition as well as against judges and courts that are supposed to deal in justice. I know many people didn't agree with Governor Brown, but I said for many years before I met him that he was a good politician. He impressed me so much so that I gave him an eagle feather that I doctored to hang in his office so that he would not forget us.

There was a time when I couldn't point to one white man I'd call my brother. Not one. Now I can call my brothers hundreds I've met and know to be honest. But they are not in politics and they are not in office. I don't want to get involved in politics, but I am interested to the extent that I realize if we're going to have peace we need to have someone speaking out for the poor people and the Indians.

Hypocritical people ask me just what it is that the Indians want. The best answer I can give them is, "What does anybody else want?" We all want exactly the same thing, to live in peace and take care of ourselves unmolested. All people want the same things: security to the extent that they know they can eat, and that they can raise their families without fear that a dictator will take their children away. They want the right to worship the Great Spirit in a way they understand. They want the same things that the Constitution provides for but never fulfills. We want to leave something for our young people that we can be proud of.

The white man is making a big mistake if he doesn't ask Indians for some of their knowledge. Everything is written down and hidden away because we don't believe in giving something for nothing. Sharing works two ways. Twenty to thirty years ago we had no white friends at all. The prophecies said that we would someday find our white brothers but they were not to be the people who signed the treaties and pushed us off our land. Spiritual gatherings between whites and Indians are the most important events in maybe one hundred years. It's the first time we've seen large spiritual gatherings that are interested in preserving all nature. Indians are beginning to be recognized for what we have to offer. Some people actually hunger for our contribution toward preserving nature.

We are the teachers now. If you come to learn, okay. If you come to teach, we don't have any openings. When you come among us, respect our customs. We respect other people's customs. We have the attitude that you're here to learn and that includes everything. We allow no drugs, no alcohol, no meditation, and no violence, and that includes in a person's thinking. We've become kind of rough; we had to in order to survive. Let us work together to bring back the spirit of this land and to heal the wounds of the Mother Earth and to make us spiritually strong. There are many places a person could start to do justice and to bring about understanding, peace, and brotherhood.

A good place to start would be to be thinking about providing land for thousands of Indians living in the slums. The white man must return our stolen land and keep the treaties. There's plenty of stolen land. There's room for all people here, providing the distribution is right. Our religion says that the land, all of Mother Earth, belongs to the Great Spirit, the Creator, and that humans are only its keepers or trustees, who are allowed to live on the soil and cultivate it. We don't think we own the land, and we certainly don't believe that anybody else can own it either. We say there's room for everyone if we all share as brothers and sisters. We all belong here in this country. We are made to live in a beautiful way.

Digging up Indian graves must stop. If you know a congressman or senator, then you'd better get busy—those people claim they represent you. So you'd better get busy if your arm's not broken and you're going around claiming to be a friend of the Indians or part Cherokee. Then you'd better put something on the dotted line before it's too late.

We Indians have to work in our own way. Non-Indians must do whatever it is that you know how to do in your own way, because we ourselves do not like being told what to do. So it's not up to me to tell you how to do your thing or what the answers are. It's up to you to tell your own chiefs and politicians and in your own way in whatever way they understand. We're not dead, any of us, until we give up, become apathetic

or disinterested, so that we become so dull-witted or intimidated that we're afraid of the truth. You tell your politicians
how they can make peace if they want peace. You tell them—
they're supposed to be working for you. They're your chiefs,
not mine. Fact is, if we had a chief like almost all of your politicians, we'd turn him over to the women and he wouldn't
be chief very long. Write to your representatives. If they get
enough letters from the general public who let them know
that they are opposed to this state of affairs, that what they're
doing is genocide, then maybe they will act.

I'm not asking you to be Indians but I am asking that all of
you return to Great Spirit's trail. Be honest and refuse to put up
with some of the things that you don't have to put up with.
How do your representatives know what you want? What's to
stop them from thinking you don't approve?

Don't ever feel guilty unless you're part of the desecration
of Mother Earth, unless you got it coming. We're not here to
make people feel guilty. We're here to wake you up. We love it
when other people start to join with us as one mind, one
thought. It's a healing thing because once you're happy, really
truly honestly happy, that's part of the healing.

If you've been living a good life and not been part of the
stealing of other people's children, if you've not been part of
stealing other people's lands, if you've not been ripping off
your neighbor, and if you've really been living as a spiritual
person, then I can tell you that you won't have anything to
worry about. There's no need to be afraid. The spiritual is
always more powerful than the physical. That's what I'm trying to tell you—the spiritual force is far greater than any force
of violence.

Wrong conditions, such as genocide against any people

and destroying nature, shouldn't exist, and I think any good Christian or Buddhist would agree with me. Some people ask what it is they can do, and then they say they can't do anything. You know—or you should know if you were raised properly and had the proper instructions—that anyone can always make a prayer. So don't tell me there's nothing that can be done. I've had young Indians in the Oklahoma prisons tell me they heard our prayers coming through the prison walls. The time for action and bringing people together and adhering to Great Spirit's law is here and now, and it's not going to wait for anybody that falls behind to catch up.

Until people learn to get along among themselves, how can they respect each other, how can they have their own self-respect, keep their treaties, and make peace? The first step in getting well for nations as well as individuals is to be honest with oneself; before we can have peace in this world we have to have understanding and compassion. I'd like to see more respect for other people's religions and other people's beliefs. The main thing that has been forgotten in the civilized world is respect.

The reason that nations and peoples cannot make peace is because they have lost their roots; many people have lost their contact with Mother Earth and only know how to destroy. Respect for self and everyone else should begin with Mother Earth. There are ways we can preserve nature, such as replanting the trees in the west where there are no trees because they have been clear-cut, and there is nothing to hold the soil and stop the floods. This would make lots of work for people including Native Americans and help our economy as well as our environment.

TURNING IT OVER TO THE GREAT SPIRIT

I've seen poor people sleeping under bridges and on the streets. People told me they had no home to go to. I think that a society that allows this is crummy, shameless, and I think we are all part of it. I'm the worst for allowing these kinds of conditions in my homeland. This is my land, but not my government. I am the worst for allowing it in my land. On some of the reservations my people are starving. Some of our people are being displaced, kicked right out of their hogans and right off their land, and we're allowing it to happen. Yes, we're all guilty.

Some of my people might use different measures, such as reoccupying a piece of land they know is rightfully theirs. Sometimes they walk all the way across the country to try to get somebody somewhere to listen. But there's been so much warfare and genocide against us that now we're not going to those places anymore. We've turned it over to the Great Spirit.

Do you know why I'm proud to be an Indian? Because even with all this going on we still don't hate anyone, even when they fought us at a place called Wounded Knee. I've also been on both ends of the gun. My grandfather, a traditional chief, was murdered by soldiers and agency police. It's not part of the Indian nature to hate and it's not the way of the Great Spirit to hold hate and malice against anyone. The fact is we have helped many people, including non-Indians.

On the Politics of Ancestry

Don't tell me you're American if you or your ancestors were French or English or whatever, because that's gonna rub me the wrong way. We think we're the Americans. We've been told that the white people are Americans, and we're nobody or savages. So let's get it back in its proper context. We're not ashamed of what we are, and we do not see why anybody else should have to be ashamed.

We don't believe everyone is alike. We're all different. Some are brown, some are black, but we teach that differences should be respected. When you come among us, don't be ashamed of whatever you are; then we can meet and start to reestablish your own self-respect and you'll have respect for us. In other words, it's a fair exchange. You can learn to walk proud and be real people. But be proud in the right way and humble in the presence of a ceremony and the Great Spirit's way of life.

Another thing we don't like is when someone comes along saying that their great grandmother was a Cherokee princess. Many people are wannabe Indians; if you aren't Indian, don't go around claiming you are because it will catch up with you someday. A person can state what they are and not be ashamed or misrepresent themselves in any way. At this time there about two or three million Cherokees. Do not call yourself an Indian if you believe your great grandmother was a Cherokee princess. Have a little respect, and understand that there have never been Cherokee princesses. I'm always tactful and try to be as courteous as I can. I just make a joke, and I tell those with Cherokee ancestor princesses that my great grandfather really got around. So do not claim you are an Indian unless you are in fact. In this way we get to know each other, and if you are not a registered Indian, that's okay too.

I could have been enrolled but I prefer not to be. This reminds me of a young Indian in Louisiana. The government said his people were extinct but I found that there are ten thousand of them not recognized by the government living in

New Orleans and out in the swamps. They don't have roll numbers and a lot of them are full-bloods. They were trying to be recognized by the federal government to get money, but the young Indian wanted to know why should the government tell him he's Indian? And I agree with him. A roll number is like a prison number that was originally given to our people when they were rounded up. Our people were given white names because the whites couldn't pronounce the American Indian names.

I've spent my entire life without a roll number. I know who my relations are, and can prove my lineage. I'm a traditional Indian even if I might not look like it to some people. The tribe I come from, the Cherokee, are more slender and not quite as dark as the desert Indians out west. In the past, Cherokees were lighter in the first place, and we don't hold the blood. If we mix a little bit with the whites or the blacks or somebody else for one generation, our color is gone; the children come out looking white or black. I'm a mixed-blood myself.

I would say there are seven million Indians in this country who don't have roll numbers. Some Indian tribes issued their own passports. Why do we have to look to the government to prove who we are? It's not the complexion that matters, but rather where your heart is and which way the blood flows. That's the first thing we will ask you when you come among us because we want to know which side you are on.

I think we need to spend less time criticizing others and each other, and more in cleaning up our own act and standing on our own feet. I've never had time for stuff like feeling sorry for myself or waiting to be recognized. We have to be happy with whatever we are and to complete our tasks in life. Cherokees are light enough that we can pass among white people, infiltrate them. I did for a little while, and they didn't know I was an Indian. Then I'd go back to the tribe and make a report. I guess that was part of the reason I was born this way.

I'm one of the wild ones; I call others who don't know the teachings the lost ones because they lost their trail somewhere. And as far as who's an Indian and who's not an Indian, I remember the days when we could know our own by the way a person walked, certain marks on the body, and certain mannerisms. You could tell if you knew how, even if they were blue-eyed and mixed-blood. It's something no one can take away from you unless you yourself give it up.

I remember one famous Cherokee singer, an Eastern Cherokee Indian. I know some of his relations. They're full-blood Indian, but he's not. Nowadays he's not an Indian because somebody called him a white man. The poor guy—I'm sorry for him because he took it into himself. I've been called everything. I just tell them, "Thank you for the information," and walk away. In other words, we can't spend too much time feeling sorry for ourselves. I was born this way and I'm going to be this way for the rest of my natural life, so for anybody who doesn't like it, that's too bad.

All of Us Belong Here

The Great Spirit intended for all of us to be here or we would not be here. But the Spirit does intend that we should live in a certain way. No one should hate anyone else, because what affects one affects all. If the white people get hurt, we get hurt. If we get hurt, somebody else is going to need us before they know it, and they'll be hurt one way or another too. They might need us to help put things back in order so that the seasons come in time, so that the rains not be too hard, so that all the volcanoes don't erupt. And in this land, only the American Indians are the caretakers of the land.

We all belong here. There's room for everyone. I've heard the propaganda that there are too many people, and from some young people, which disappoints me. This is propaganda, and of all the places I have been, the lies are the worst here. With proper distribution and consideration of Mother Earth, there is plenty for everyone. A famous ecologist, Buckminster Fuller, and his niece, lived with us for a while. Buckminster Fuller is a great man besides being a scientist, and he can throw statistics out a mile a minute, which I cannot do. When I was in Canada at a big spiritual meeting, he proved with numbers in a way that all the people there could understand the same things that we Indians have been trying to say. He proved that with the proper use and distribution of resources and people there would be no pollution and plenty for everyone. This would require that people have a heart and mind to do things in the right kind of way. This country could yet feed the world if certain people had a mind to do so instead of making war.

Our cause is the same as your cause: to survive, to get back to the spirit again so that our people can be strong. The main thing I'm doing is to bring a message that peace and economic security are possible. The message I'd like for all people around the world to know is that American Indians are a peaceful people and that we only want to live in brotherhood and peace with all the other people of the earth.

I can understand why in the early days white people felt they had to exterminate the Indians, because they wanted to own the land. But I cannot understand why white people continue to harm their own people by dumping harmful chemicals in the water and spraying deadly poisons in the air. Now there's hardly a safe place to swim, much less water fit to drink. The air is filthy too. It just doesn't make sense.

We can understand generally why people don't give a damn about the American Indian in these times. But I don't understand many things white people do today, such as lack of concern for their neighbors, people in their own families, or people down the street. I have seen old ladies in New York with packs on their backs walking the streets. I thought they were hitch-hiking, but my New York friends said that they were old pensioners who didn't have money to pay the rent. I asked about where they sleep, and my friends said they sleep in doorways. And this is the financial capital of the world, and them bragging about how rich they are and how they got that way off their stolen loot. It makes me angry, makes my blood boil, when I see people being abused, thrown out of their homes, because they can't afford to pay rent. At that point the races cease to exist. We Indians believe in maintaining our culture, but we don't go over to our neighbor, throw them off their land, and watch them go hungry.

There was the time that young warriors were coming back from Wounded Knee and arrest warrants were out on some of them. Some had been hurt and I had to go to San Francisco to take care of a few of them. They were living in the home of an elderly white lady, but there was no food in the house and she had three daughters she was putting through college and high school at that time. She was crying. This happened right after Governor Ronald Reagan started the welfare cuts. She had lost her job because she was on one of those programs. She was over seventy years old and she was crying because there was no food in the house. She asked me at that time, "What are the poor white people going to do?" I said, "Lady, I'm not a politician, and I can't lie to you, so I can't tell you about those kinds of things."

In the meantime our young men went out—we had a little money that time—and got groceries and filled her kitchen with food. The next time I saw that old lady, she wasn't crying. She was working over in the AIM office in San Francisco I think it was. Pretty scrappy old lady.

In the old days when the tribe was traveling and there was hunger, the chief and the medicine man had to eat last after the others had been fed. Now how would it be if your politicians had such a system? Me and my wife, Spotted Fawn, never saved a dime in our lives. We never had a savings account because I never got the hang of it when there's people out there a few miles away on the reservation hungry. I'd take carloads of food when I'd go out there. How could someone save money when someone else just a short distance away, their own people, is starving to death? I know there are some people who could, but I just never got the hang of it. When I worked on the freight trains, many times I gave my lunch to the hobos. I also tried to get those people out of the cold by finding an empty boxcar for them. I've never been charged with any crime, but I say I've committed a few: fed some hungry people, helped some people in need.

Admonitions for the Present and Future

The battle we are fighting is for all people and not merely for us Indians. The next thing you know they will be treating you like an Indian, stealing your land, stealing your children. You are not going to like it; you are going to scream so that they can hear you a long way off. But who's gonna help you? I'd like to help you.

The worst enemy of all is violence, and non-Indians are going to be the victims of it unless they put their minds and hearts together. White men have become addicted to violence, and war is the civilized people's worst pollution. They should learn from history: they are fat now, rich, but they have not looked within themselves.

I don't think genocide is right, regardless of who it's directed at. Many people do not want to admit to anything that doesn't sound good to them. When I get around those people I feel kinda sorry for them that they're so dumb; they may be next and they might not know it. I don't wish that on them, but they will be. It looks like they are willing to see the nation fall apart. There is more crime now than ever before as people go crazy. The jails are overflowing and they can't build prisons fast enough. Guarding prisoners has become one of the biggest industries in this country. They're still pushing us and now they're pushing against each other, committing crimes of violence and genocide against each other with no shame.

We have much to share, and many things will have to be put back into their proper order for us to survive on this Mother Earth. We are at the edge of terrible times right now. There will be a famine because of weather changes, but the politicians will send food to other people to help support dictatorships rather than give it to you. A big revolution will be arranged so that they can pit whoever they can against each other. They have no understanding of the weather changes or anything else.

If you could ever put your minds together as one you'd have the key to how there could be peace and plenty for everyone on this Mother Earth. That is the power of the Spirit, what we try to teach. That way all prophecy would be fulfilled with good, and other things would not have to happen. You would have to think about peace, and then do it, at least in your thinking. I've seen a Thunder Nation rising and this time for good. Think about what you're doing. Think about your neighbors and the American Indians. Are you watching them go down the drain? If we cannot live on this land, you're not going to. It's already been guaranteed to us, and I don't mean living as somebody's subjects.

Everything turns in circles. If we do good work, it comes back to us, even in our thinking. Every word should be a prayer. If enough people put their minds together as one, there would be no wars, no unemployment. There would be peace in the world.

Anyone can be a spiritual person by maintaining internal harmony and compassion. When you maintain internal harmony and compassion, the answers would come to you, you would know what to do to cope with problems and how to apply yourselves to make life better for others. When you meet someone, you should always meet them as a friend, as a brother. Think how you can help that person to feel better or get them to smile. People need to feel free to smile and do their own thing, live their own lives. Oppression and restrictions on people—as long as they do not infringe on someone else's rights—must end. People should not be free to destroy, but rather to create. In so doing, they will create good feelings and brotherhood.

When we come to power, it does not mean that we want people to return to Europe or whatever, like some people might expect. We recognize our teachings that tell us that the white people need us, and we need white people and black people and all other kinds of people. Do you know that it would take at least one hundred years, and likely many more, to clean up the mess—the rivers, replanting trees and so forth—that's been made here? You know we would need all the help we can get. But we are going to tighten up our immigration laws because they have been far too lax. We are going to take all the politicians who made laws against the Indians and the poor to the east coast and ask them if they can swim. We will not let certain people out—the good people who want to live in peace and a genuine kind of balanced prosperity where we can help each other. We need all the good ones. We don't need the bums, the treaty breakers, and the thieves.

Traveling and communicating with people is good. Years ago no white person really wanted to hear what an Indian had to say. But now some do and this is what gives us hope for the future, that there will be a future for our children and our grandchildren. What we wish for ours is the same thing we hope for yours. *Ho.*

NOTE

1. In this case, the "spiritual warriors" Rolling Thunder mentions are references to powerful medicine men of his caliber or higher.

CHAPTER SEVEN

Ruby Mountains in northeastern Nevada.

Rolling Thunder and Sun Rising, 1996.

The Great Spirit's Trail

"At one time, original peoples all over the world had the same nature religion that came from Father Sun and Mother Earth."

Even though our entire lives are dedicated to prayer and practice, many people have told me—including supposedly educated people—that they didn't know the Indians had a religion. Our religion can't be put in a book, or even an entire library, because it includes everything that has life. Everything, including the rocks and the mountains, have spirits.

I explained once to some missionaries that we have a bible. It's in the clouds up there in that blue sky and in the rocks, if you can learn to read it. That bible would also be in a stream of pure water or in the words of a waterfall, like in the place where I was raised. It's said the old-time Indians knew the meaning of every twig that moved, and they could pick up a rock and read it. Some still do.

I've read the Bible, the Koran, the Kaballah, and the Buddhist books once. I can remember anything when I read it once because I read it with a clear mind. I think everybody should read those books, but I had to put them away because none contain the meanings of the Mother Earth, the Father Sun, and the Great Mystery. They are limited, but that doesn't mean they're all bad. There are many good things in all of them, and I enjoyed reading them. But as far as reading them again like the missionaries told me to do, what the hell do I want to do that for when I can quote the things? There's good and bad in each of them, but there are some things that might have been changed a little bit in the translations. Certain things were modified, twisted, misinterpreted, or like the Dead Sea Scrolls, that were taken out and buried in the sand. Religious teaching has to come from an original and pure source, from the Mother Earth itself, the Father Sun, and the Grandmother Moon, and none of them have that.

I don't like the word "religion" because it's misused. It came from an ancient Latin word "regio," which meant "to regiment the people." The church and the state got together and they both found it to their advantage to control the minds of the people. Then they needed a word for it so they called it "religion." So when I say Indian religion, it's really incorrect because the Great Spirit's way is not about regimenting people's minds.

At one time Great Spirit's way of life, or the nature religion in its pure form, extended around the world. When we go back far enough there are no differences among the ancient teachings of the spiritual ways of life. I know this because when I met with other original peoples around the world, I could read their emblems. I could understand why they built their temples and why they danced in a circle.

Traditional Indians live close to nature and with nature regardless of all other things swirling around them trying to consume them. We live our lives based on the tribal way teachings and of the ancient civilizations of this land still known to us. We know how to live with nature and that's what we teach.

We have no religion in the way that most non-Indians

understand it. Spirituality has nothing to do with holiness and churches. The spiritual way of life is twenty-four hours a day, and includes everything that has life. My spiritual way of life is out there in those beautiful trees that are surviving, the sun overhead, and the sky is the roof of my temple. The river flowing and the ocean are part of my bible and my religion.

The Meaning of the Circle

I'd like to tell you a little bit about the meaning of the circle that was known to all ancient peoples when they followed the nature religion. The ancient people knew that everything, even the universe, is composed of a circle. The universe travels in a circle; all life is composed of circles. All original peoples recognized the circle at one time.

We talk in a circle; we always come back to the starting point. The circle is sacred to us because it is the emblem of our native way of life. Everything that's happened before, happens again. Nations too rise and fall, live and die, the same as individuals. Nothing is perfect and nothing is permanent in this life except for the Great Spirit, the Creator over all.

You'll see the circle in the ancient graveyards in Ireland. Sometimes a cross was placed there later, but even then the circle wasn't lost. Now the circle has been broken and almost lost. People are divided and getting ready for the last big war. These are the reasons I speak out.

We recognize the circle in all things. All matter, all life is composed of circles. The life of all living things extends down through the sun and the lightning that charges the air, the clouds, and then the earth. Life comes back to us in the water we drink and the food we eat. We call it the life force, and the civilized world's scientists probably call it electrical energy; it is in all living things, including the plants. It's what we deal with, this life force. We don't think that this God, as you call him, or as we say the Grandfather or Great Spirit, is hiding behind a cloud somewhere or that you have to wait until death to know him. The Great Spirit lives in all things that have life—animals, plants, birds, rocks. The Great Spirit is in all of us according to our desires.

On Conjuring Up and Fighting the Devil

Foreign ways were brought to this land. I call them foreign because they didn't recognize nature and the rights of anyone else, and because they are different, with only a heaven and a hell. We don't threaten people with hells and devils. We don't say "sin," but rather "wrongdoing." We don't like to think of gruesome things like people burning in hell forever and ever. That's the kind of mentality and anti-spirituality that was conjured up and then brought over here because certain groups of people needed a way to control others. Some of their rulers wanted such a thing so that the masses of people, even the little children, could be regimented and ruled through fear. Europeans conjured up the devil in 1152 AD.

That devil was over here at one time. Ecknock belonged to a tribe that was very quarrelsome. Finally, he got his own tribe together and made war on the surrounding tribes. He established a great empire in the area of the Grand Canyon. Now this is not European history or fairy-tale American history—this is real American history. So after he made other tribes join together, they kept making war. But you know, that kind of stuff might work on the Indian for just a little while. Some of his own tribe rebelled and the other tribes all joined them and they put the devil to death.

But Ecknock couldn't really be killed because he had so much evil power. So he went to Europe and the Holy Land where they conjured him up again: if you believe in something and believe in it long enough, it will come into being. In other words, the devil was welcomed again. He came into being again and was written into their books and bragged about and exploited.

The people who broke people on racks during the Inquisition and burned witches at the stake said they were Christians. Anyone could be a witch, women especially. Once they were denounced, they'd always confess, especially once they'd pull out their fingernails or started to burn them. In one place in Germany there were only two women left in the town when they got through burning witches.

The people who said they were Christians brought their devil along with them when they came here across the Great Waters. So the devil is here again after being brought over by the pilgrims, the most evil-minded people in the world. Our immigration laws were quite lax then. The first pilgrims were real bad: they burned witches on Sunday, whipped people for kissing on Sunday, put people in stocks, and bad things started to happen here again.

You can have the white Christian devil, because we don't believe in scaring little children and threatening them with the devil or hell if they aren't good. Children threatened in this way start to live in fear and grow up paranoid, or have hangups of some kind. Living in fear and paranoia comes from old puritan teachings and concepts of the world. These notions of the devil and hell are carryovers from other religions and governments, and I think it explains why a lot of people today do the things they do.

But we Indians have fired the white Christian devil. I don't agree with him, don't like him, and the fact is, I had a fight with him once and I think I whipped him. There's always one or two good Christians who get upset when I start talking about beating up on their devil, and I don't know why. But isn't that what we're all trying to do? We'll teach you how, we're the people who know how. I really had a fight with that devil and I admit it was my own fault, because I'd been bragging to some of my people that as old as I was I could still move and whip the devil. And I shouldn't have.

I was looking into a problem with a young Cherokee girl who was bothered by bad spirits. She had been a Christian and she was a mess. All her life she had been trying to please the white man, the only teachings she had ever had. She had been drinking and doping, and marrying white men, and she had made a wreck out of herself. She was suffering terribly, wasting away, both physically and mentally. She looked ten years older than what she should have looked because Indians don't age very fast when they live the good life. She was a good girl but she didn't know one Indian spiritual thing. So she wanted me to look into what was bothering her. I had a smoke, and it wasn't marijuana, and did other things to prepare myself that night before I want to bed.

During the night this thing, a huge being in the form of a man, appeared there by my bedside. He looked like he was made from little grains of rice or sawdust pressed together into the form of a man. I knew he was composed of all the sins of the world pressed together into the body of a man maybe eight feet tall. That was the first time I'd met the bird, but I knew it was that devil. Evil vibrations came out of him and he stank. He was so evil that I couldn't help myself—I jumped up and hit him with a left to his face, and part of his face flew off. Then I hit him with a right to his stomach and part of his stomach flew off. But he was still standing there.

I backed off a minute or two. I thought, now this is going to be quite a job, might take two or three days to bring that old boy down. When an Indian has to fight, he goes all out and there is no such thing as a fair fight. I thought, well, I'll use my feet, my elbows, and my knees. I'll bite a little and whatever else it takes. I must have been thrashing around terribly in the bed because my woman started yelling, "What's the matter?"

She woke me up finally. It was so real it took me a little while to come to. When I finally came to and was propped up on one elbow, I told her, "I just had a fight with the devil and I think I whipped him."

And she said, "Now isn't that silly. Don't you realize there's more power in your eagle feather than in your fist?"

Well, I knew that all the time. Every Indian who knows anything knows that. I knew that but I'd never tried to go by it before. She turned over and went back to sleep. I lay flat on my back the rest of the night, and kept thinking over and over, "more power in my eagle feather than in my fist...more power in my eagle feather than in my fist." By morning I had it down pretty good.

The next time I meet that ol' boy, I'll wipe him out. I know it because I'll use my eagle feather. I don't worry about him too much, but I don't like what he does to people. From what they tell me, he's the one who causes people to think bad things and do bad things. I think that's why they pray and sing. They always tell me they're trying to defeat the evil spirits. But if you don't get ahold of him and send him back where he comes from, I will have to do it for you. I also know for a fact that he doesn't want any Indians on that reservation they call hell, and he especially doesn't want me.

In the white man's Christian hell, it's said that people are burning and burning forever and ever. Why do people go there? It might be that they murdered somebody without authority to do so, or didn't pay their taxes on time, or maybe didn't contribute to the church. Maybe they weren't in the right political clique, or believed in some other kind of social system and they got called a communist. Or they believed in tribalism, or got caught stealing. Maybe they drank too much or cheated on their wives. But they would not go to hell for breaking Indian treaties. Indians don't have to worry about going to their hell because old Satan has orders out to all the preachers and undertakers, and even Saint Peter: "Don't send me any Indians down here. I have enough troubles as it is, and I especially don't want that guy who's called Rolling Thunder, who conjures up the rain."

No One Has a Monopoly on the Great Spirit

I do believe people should have a choice about where they go after they die. For anyone involved with treaty breaking, I think the Christian hell is a good place for them. Anyone who believes in the Bureau of Indian Affairs way, that's where they ought to go. I think the other place, the Christian heaven, is real nice for people who want it that way.

Christians are always looking for something wrong with us. We Indians have never claimed to have a monopoly on the Great Spirit. Only your churches claim that you have to get baptized in a certain way or you go to hell. We're not better than anyone, but we know the way that fits us, the way that came from this land and the way that still fits this land. We have always been a free thinking kind of people. We don't go along with those foreign beliefs at all. We believe anyone can use Great Spirit's power regardless of race, religion, or wherever they came from.

There are many trails to follow. We are not fanatical about our spiritual way of life and we do recognize that there are many others—Christians, Buddhists, Moslems, Jews—and we don't say one is better than the other, or that we are better than they are. We will not lower ourselves or restrict our thinking and knowledge into ignorant differences and patterns. We leave that for others. We don't tell anyone that if they don't become an Indian, they will go to hell. We don't want to imitate ignorant people.

Divisions are made by governments and religions, each one claiming to know the right trail or a better one than the other. I'm not anti-Christian even though I've never been a Christian. I'm not anti-Buddhist either. One thing we don't need are missionaries, dictators, or Indian agents. We're very happy with the way we live; we have the sovereign right that we're born with and that Indians everywhere are returning to.

Maybe half of all Indians have converted to Christianity, but today many of those are returning to the old ways. The spirit of this land and the power of our people are coming back to us. Many other religions are good and it's not proper for me to criticize them, unless they have injured me in some way. I'm not entitled to criticize the other religions that came across the water from the east or the west. I'm satisfied that originally when they were practiced in a true way, they were all good.

Some people think their way is the only way to live, and

they don't realize that other people have different customs, different ways. Our way works for us, and has for thousands of years, and many of us have no intention of changing it. People can't understand why Indians are not overly enthused when the missionaries come around. They can't understand why those "poor savages" don't want this good thing crammed down their throats. No one has a right to come along and tell you how to live your life. Your life is your own, granted to you by the Great Spirit. As an individual you decide the way you want to live that fits you. The minute someone starts deciding for you, they take your right. Each person, no matter what race or color, is born with a certain sovereign right, which is theirs until they sign it away or give it up.

I don't want to contest anybody about their religion. Everyone is entitled to follow the way they know best, but nobody has a monopoly on the Great Spirit. Nobody owns the Great Spirit. The same Creator created all of us and meant for all of us to live in peace.

People need to get back to recognizing and honoring individual rights. If they did, they'd get back to the natural way. We are on this Mother Earth to make things better for each other and to help each other. That's what it's all about really. People have become too self-centered in this civilization and that's the trouble I find among many of the whites.

On Money

Missionaries try to tell us that we worship the same god and that we're all the same. That's whitewash propaganda. We do not worship the same god. The god of "civilized" society is the dollar, and it's been that way a long time. They will kill for it, break treaties for it, go all the way across the ocean to conjure up a war to make a few little dollars. They'll do anything for that dollar, so that proves their god is the dollar. It's not the same god as ours, so missionaries telling Indians that we worship the same god is an insult.

The difference is as wide as the day and the night, as wide as the ocean. There is no similarity between our spiritual way of life and modern American society. Money doesn't impress me—money is not my god. I have faith that whatever I need will be provided and it is. No amount of money can buy me. Our way is a different kind of way, which includes sharing what we have and never having saved a dime. If we help others, then help comes back to us. That's the way it works. In our Native spiritual way of life, we're activist people. We don't believe in sitting and doing nothing or putting money in a plate.

Another example of whitewash propaganda is when white people say that money is the root of all evil. Money in itself is not evil. When I think of money I think of how many people it will feed. It's where it comes from and how it's used that really counts. We're not very good at counting money, but we're very good at spending it. We spend it as fast as we get it on foolishness like food and building materials. Some white people think about how many guns and bullets money would buy.

Success to us has a different meaning than it does to these foreign people. Yes, they are foreign people until they learn the way of this land. If I have money, I turn around and give it away or use it to buy food or herbs. It's only good for exchange, and it's too bad that they've got us dependent on it now. If they had just left our people alone, we'd be all right. Our people would be a wealthy people, maybe not so much in money but in a way that is really worth something.

I don't think it's right that people organizing spiritual meetings charge money, but who is going to buy gas and other things for the elders to travel to these meetings? The richer white people usually paid my way to meetings where I would talk. I don't charge anything for the Indians attending these meetings. Unfortunately, people do have to make a living. I don't think it's right either that the doctors have to charge. Nothing is free, even for poor people.

The white people do have more money; they have an economy and we Indians do not. White people have rarely been generous to the Indians. They'll pay lots of money for huge Buddhist and Christian palaces, for big temples and churches, but when they get to the Indian, that shack out there is good enough. Starving is good enough for Indians.

People can be more successful in their own lives if they're honest rather than putting the make on somebody, like kicking old widow women out of their homes. Greed leads to bad luck coming back to you. The problem is that many people don't believe in that anymore. Anyone can be a spiritual person regardless of ethnic background once they get over their egos and greediness; in other words, people become spiritual when they become their own masters.

We are poor too, out there in the desert where we live in shacks, tipis, and wickiups. We're considered about the poorest in the country. But it's like I told some rich people in Beverly Hills: in our shacks we're happier than they are and that's something their money can't buy. Don't feel sorry for the poor Indians and all that stuff from the past. We are happy people if we have a roof over our heads, our families together, good health, and are able to live in peace and not be hassled or molested. We take care of ourselves very well.

We do our best to help ourselves and to help others. That is our spiritual way of life, the basis of it. Every day of our lives we try. We walk softly upon the Mother Earth, which means living in tune with nature and living as self-sufficiently as possible. Our Indian religion is an activist religion, one we have to live every day, not just one day a week.

Indians and Christianity

The Great Spirit tells us that in life there are many choices to be made about our paths, but there is only one path where an Indian will be truly happy and that is Great Spirit's trail. This trail may look steep and rough compared to others. But each day we have a choice and we are supposed to live every day better than the one before to get to a higher spiritual level. We always have to choose between good and evil, and we have to choose wisely. Many of our young people stray off into the cities, and try so-called modern life. They may try different pathways in life: assimilation, booze and drugs, foreign religions. But when they get hurt, they return home to their original ways.

I've never belonged to a foreign religion and never will. Some of us were dedicated to remaining true to our own like Great Spirit instructed, although at one time I did try to please the white man. Finally I gave it up. I wasn't happy and they weren't pleased with me that way. I said to hell with it, I'm going to please myself and go back to my people. And I did. I went back to my home country in Oklahoma and found them in the woods still holding out with the morale high—no drinking, no fighting at the stomp dances, and everything real good.

The main criticism I have to make to all of you, especially

you good white people, is that you've become too apathetic. In other words, if you think it's going to cure anything to go out and smoke dope, or sit and meditate, or sing in your churches and then put money in the plate, you're on the wrong trail. It's not going to cure one thing. But I'd like to go a little further than that, and say that you are not concerned about your brothers. Whenever we sit back and watch our brothers get hurt, we're just as guilty as the one doing it. Apathy is part of the same sickness as violence against people. Apathetic people are too self-centered. They don't even know who their neighbors are or if they get along all right. They've even lost respect for themselves.

I know there must be good Christians who see bad things going on. What's the matter with them? When the priests, rabbis, and other religious leaders see people hurting themselves and others and think they can't do anything, it's anti-spiritual, a work of the evil spirits. There are some religious leaders who try to take care of their people, which they should do. I don't have a bone to pick with anyone like that. I like to see action coming from good people, real spiritual people.

William Penn had a healthy and peaceful attitude toward the Indians; he got along with them and believed in treating them fairly. The Quaker people were the first among the white people who would give us any help at all. They helped us when we had no lawyers, no one to speak for us. There have been others since.

In fact, I have many friends among Christians. I had a friend, just a young fella, who was a Methodist preacher in the little town of Carlin. He got to talking to me and would read the Bible to me. He'd want my interpretation, the Indian interpretation of those scriptures, and he'd take notes. I guess he took it to his church though, and they fired him. So I tell people to watch out: we thoroughly contaminate people everywhere we go. I had another friend there, a Baptist minister. He liked to get together with me every chance he had, but he was a little older and maybe a little wiser. He said the things I told him were too heavy for the public, so he didn't talk about them in certain places, and they didn't fire him.

That Jesus they talk about was an activist too. He was a great man, a great healer. He had compassion, but he wasn't the kind to sit back, go to church on Sunday, and then disregard wrongdoings the rest of the week. He was a militant. He put fear of their own evil doings into the hearts and minds of those money changers in the temple. He was the greatest kind of warrior, a spiritual warrior. He was a warrior for peace, not any kind of a patsy like he has been portrayed, and not about to be pushed around by anybody. He also held anger, an anger against injustice.

The way I have seen it, he wouldn't have gone in there and said, "pretty please," or turned the other cheek. You know damn well he didn't. You know it as well as I know it if you've got any common sense. They'd have mopped up the floor with him. I'll tell you how it was because it's different than how you might have heard it. When he went through that door, he let out a scream and a victory whoop. About that time—there's always a wise guy around, you know—a wise guy comes over to him and really starts to tell Jesus off. The wise guy got his face slapped.

About that time the wise guy's buddies decided to help their buddy. One of these good buddies got a karate chop. Some were flying through windows and doors. Some of them got a sandal in the rear on the way out. Jesus really cleaned it up, and he stopped them. They were screaming for their lives, and the reason they got a sandal in the rear was just to emphasize, so they wouldn't forget and do it again.

I haven't done enough research yet to know why the rabbi was letting the money changers use his temple for this unholy kind of business. It's not recorded in their bible, the deal made with the local rabbi to use the temple, but I suspect that the rabbi wasn't true even to his own religion.

Missionaries have asked me whether I believe in Jesus Christ. I have told them that I believe in him and have a great respect for him. I then ask the missionaries why they lack respect for him. I'm not a Christian, yet I've got more respect for their own great teacher than they have. I think there are many misconceptions in Christian religions. I don't think that Jesus Christ wanted to die. He had to die, yes, because he found himself involved with evil people and they did him in. That man didn't want to be murdered, nor to be a martyr. He wasn't crazy. He was a great man and a great healer but they picture him spreadeagled on a cross and desecrate him.

Jesus was a good man but he was foolish. He came from this land, and was reborn there. He was sent over there because they had no great medicine people left. Their priests and rabbis, their medicine people, couldn't do anything because they had become superstitious and subservient to the state. They needed someone like him because they had lost their natural spiritual powers long before.

We had a great many medicine people here who were so powerful they could walk into a tree and become part of that tree. It was common practice among the American Indians. Jesus decided to go where he was badly needed—that was the first big mistake he made. If he had stayed home he would have been a great healer and highly honored. He was reborn over there and then they killed him. Now they—the Christians and Jewish people—try to blame each other. They point their finger at each other when they're all guilty. He should have stayed here.

Anyone can be a spiritual person. We make no distinctions. Spiritual people all look the same to us as long as they follow Great Spirit's way. There's no limitation; no one owns Great Spirit's power. The Great Spirit tells us that there are many trails but only one for the Indian people. There are no limits except in a person's own mind and spirit.

Spreading the Great Spirit's Message

Many non-Indian people these days are trying to escape or to find a new way of life that fits them. But we are not missionaries and we think that people are not supposed to tell each other how to live. We do think the time will come when some non-Indians might be allowed to learn certain things from us that would benefit them and their families. But we are not trying to force anything on anyone, nor to disturb people's ways of life.

At one time we sent people who were highly trained in our own school all over the world. I'm not going to tell you where it's at. There were six years of special training. Some of us, including me, wore business suits and neckties and went to fifty-two of the great governments all over the world, and we found one that was true. We traveled to many countries, and out of fifty-two different Christian denominations, we found one that was true. Out of fifty-two Muslim groups, we found one that was true; fifty-two different Buddhist groups and one that was true, and so on. We were looking for our brothers and sisters, wherever they might be around the world. But that job is done now. I haven't worn that suit for many years because we have other things to do.

We know what we're doing, and we know what we're looking for. We know the trail we travel, and we hope that someday there will be many of you ready to travel with us. We travel many places nowadays and we move like the whirlwind when we travel to spread the message of the Great Spirit, and how it was in the beginning all around the world. We travel to find our brothers. We never overlook our people, who are all Great Spirit's people, whatever race they come from.

Our way of life is based on an ancient culture and we're not buying anybody else's anymore. Some of the young whites who come to live with us are not permitted to stay. It's our choice: they are turned away because they still want to follow foreign religions or use drugs or alcohol. None of these things are permitted. If they want to respect our ways, they have to join us. We don't join them any more. We think it's good when people come to us to learn our ways and more about the laws of this land, but it's their choice. If they can fit themselves in with us, we treat them a lot better than their ancestors treated us. Don't think you're coming among the Indians and that you're going to make a fool out of anybody, because those days are gone.

When we traveled across the Great Waters, we were welcomed wherever we went, and far more than some places in America even today. These people were hungry for the knowledge of their past, and it was like a breath of fresh air to bring it back to them. Discovering their original way of life and culture was taken seriously, such as getting back to more respect for the Mother Earth; learning about their native plants and animals; learning the meaning of the waters and the wind, and of the many things that are lost and not taught at all in modern civilization. They had far more interest than people in America. The only groups in America where we find people with a great deal of interest are certain spiritual groups, young college students, and elderly people. There is a slow awakening underway in the American consciousness.

At Meta Tantay, we welcomed all races and nationalities, as long as they were sincere in their desire to learn the correct ways of respect and harmony. I made it clear to all whites who came that we as a people were willing to share certain aspects of the Native way. It was strictly enforced by me that all ceremonies were led only by Indian people. I made it clear to all ceremony participants that they cannot take our ceremonies, our songs, our ways, and pass them to others. No non-Native people were ever given Indian names, feathers, pipes, or other sacred objects. No non-Natives were trained to be ceremony leaders. No non-Indians may sit at our drum. I believe that as long as any Native people are being jailed, killed, sterilized, or harassed in any way for trying to follow their traditional ways of life, that no non-Native person should be allowed to have or wear our sacred objects or to be leaders of any of our ceremonies. The selling or giving away of our sacred medicine, the selling of our ceremonies, the selling of our sacred objects—all of these thing must stop. But I will not be a part of encouraging violence on these people. The Great Spirit will take care of all who make false claims, sell, or disrespect our ways.

Many traditional elders today are distressed by the hundreds of non-Native people taking Indian names and objects. Sacred pipes, sweat lodge ceremonies, crystals, eagle feathers, peyote, and other sacred objects are being sold and given out by and to nonqualified people at many gatherings. I myself have never been a party to the selling of feathers, pipes, medicine bags, or other sacred objects, nor have I given any to non-Natives. I have spoken out many times to non-Natives that if they have feathers, they should give them to a Native person as they have no right to possess them, and non-Natives are not ready to understand the power within at this time.

When you are among the Indians, you go by our customs. We respect non-Indian religions and customs whenever we travel among you. Everyone is tested when they go into an Indian camp, nowadays especially. One of the tests might be that a person is taken to where some feathers are hanging on the wall to see if the person will touch it before invited. Most of the time people do not know when they are tested.

We don't want people coming to our ceremonies drunk or doped up. We are going to lead the way, show them how. We're going to help them when we're properly invited. Don't ever drink or dope when you go into spiritual things. Go in with a clean body and a clean mind so that you don't suffer later on or make yourself worse.

Ceremonies

A ceremony in the Indian way can be anywhere and involve any number of people. A person alone can have a ceremony when she makes a prayer to the Creator. A ceremony can be with a group, with whatever name or denomination you want to call it, at any time of the day or night. We have different ceremonies that keep our lives in order. You don't have to be an Indian to have ceremonies. You don't even have to do the things the same way because what fits one might not fit another.

We have ceremonies in which we give thanks for all the

good things placed here for our benefit. We learn about our connections with the plants, animals, rocks, mountains, and all things through our ceremonies and prayers. People in the cities ought to go out into nature from time to time because it is more difficult to have ceremonies in the big cities, but the Great Spirit is always there.

We have to approach the Great Spirit in a humble way. Certain people wanted to make a movie about me as if I were a god, but I wouldn't have it. In our spiritual way of life, we realize we're not gods. We don't want anyone kneeling down and kissing our feet. We approach the Great Spirit humbly because his power is the reason for our being here.

I'll tell you a little bit about my tribe. We had a seven-sided medicine house. The ceremony to the fire took place once every seven years and had to be started with seven different types of wood native to the area.

The Cherokee pipe ceremony is different than some of the Plains tribes' pipe ceremonies. With the Cherokees, a woman brought the pipe to the men, but she was more like a mermaid. She didn't have sexual relations with any of them; it would have been impossible anyway, because she was a mermaid and lived in the water.

We sing a particular song when we carry the drum from the dance back to the village. We beat the drum all the way back to the village while singing the song to put the drum away. Our people always have respect for the elders so when the chief or the medicine man rides into the camp, they always get out the drum and sing the chief's honoring song.

We have sweat lodges, one for the men and one for the women. We don't go in together. Some Indians nowadays will have mixed sweats, but we do ours the old way, the original way. One time we built the men's lodge too close to the women's lodge, and the men's lodge just went to pieces, but the women's lodge was still in good condition. So we built the new lodge for the men out of sight of the women's lodge and it was all right.

If you go into the sweat lodge or into any of our ceremonies, you have to get away from the language of "I want." Don't use it. There are a great many other things you should know as well. When non-Indians come among Native peoples to monkey around with spiritual things, they are lost. Once two young fellas ran screaming out of a sweat lodge. They couldn't take even five minutes of the heat, but it didn't bother the rest of us.

We don't go into sweat lodges and other ceremonies with a dirty body or dirty mind. I take a bath before I go into a sweat to get the most out of it. A lot of good spiritual power is generated in there. I've heard the universe sing, even after our singing stopped: that's how powerful some of our ceremonies and sweat lodges are. When we go into a sweat, it's a sacred ceremony and we should have no other kinds of thoughts in our minds. Red-hot rocks are right in the middle and we pour cold water on them. That heat hits you right in the face; if you aren't ready for it, it will knock you down. We don't make a mistake of comparing it to a sauna—ours is hot. Some people get scalded badly if they have even one bad thought.

I tell people too who come to my ceremonies to watch their thinking. Some say they like to come there to learn. Well, okay, I think everybody's entitled to learn as long as they can listen. We don't want anyone to get hurt. The person running the sweat lodge might walk around and say that certain people can't go in. Certain white people have felt insulted. But whoever is running that ceremony has a way of knowing, and he can smell you and he can see through you, and you better believe it. He might be trying to do something good for you so that you don't get hurt because our sweats are for real.

We consider the sun as our father. The highest vibrations of the earth are in the morning when that sun is rising. We believe the morning is the best time to pray, when everything is coming to life again. When the sun rises it's supposed to be a new day and all the cares, all the problems of the past, are put behind us; new life is waking up and the birds start to sing in the morning. It's the sun that makes the winds blow, that brings the rain to water our gardens, and causes the trees to grow. We realize that all the energy of the earth comes from the sun. We realize just like all ancient people all over the earth that without that sun there could be no life upon the earth, and that is why we do not go outside during an eclipse of the sun. We do not watch as the sun dies, but stay in our lodges until the sun comes back to life and then go out and give thanks for the sun.

We have a ceremony at sunrise to welcome the Great Spirit back to the earth. The sun is one of the Great Spirit's most powerful emblems. At sunrise we form a circle in the desert and sing the welcome song, a sacred song to welcome the Great Spirit. It's the same song we sing to welcome back our young people when they've wandered out into that other world, get tired of it, and come home to us. We give thanks to the Creator for placing the sun. The best medicine in the world is the Creator and the sun when it rises in the morning.

So it is too that we remember and give thanks for the Mother Earth and for all the bird, animal, and plant life placed here that provides food for us. We give thanks for each other, the women, the babies, the warriors, and we ask always for the return of the earth. We also offer thanks to the stars in the sky that guide our way. Some of them are great warriors gone on.

We recognize the feminine principle of life. You have to listen to both the female and male. Even in our culture some people pray to the sun and forget to pray to the moon. The sun is male and the moon is female. The moon controls the water, the tides of the ocean, the rain which makes the crops grow, the women's cycle, our bodies, since they're mostly water, and our thinking. You can't pray to the sun and forget to pray to the moon. It's part of traditional Indian religion to work with both forces. Sometimes Grandmother Moon is very lonely because people will pray when the sun rises but they forget the importance of the moon.

There's a great power in Grandmother Moon, especially at the time of the full moon. You have probably heard of lunatics or moon madness from people over in Europe who learned about those things a long time ago. They seem to always want to dwell on the bad things. There's good and bad in all things, especially if you bring that condition about yourself. If you're looking for the bad, you will find it because that is what relates to you. But there's also good in Grandmother Moon. She has great power to heal wounds, heavy hearts, and the mind disturbed for any reason.

Before you enter your lodge at night, stop and give thanks to the Grandmother. Even when you can't see her because of too much smog and clouds, she is still up there. If you call on the Grandmother in the right way, you can feel better immediately. You can ask her for your peace of mind. Now don't make a long drawn-out prayer, or ask for a million dollars, please. Just ask her for your peace of mind in a few words. You can also ask for peace of mind for others who are dear to you.

Notice how much better and more peacefully you might sleep at night.

On Working Against and With Spirits

Evil spirits are those that have passed on and didn't live a good life on this earth. They're caught between this world and the world where they belong. There are others who died before their time by violence, and who may have brought the violence on themselves. Many people are not ready when they cross over, and sometimes become lost between. But people who have lived a bad life are most of the evil spirits I am talking about, the ones used to cause mischief. There is an evil spirit who has a hog's face and a great big belly. I've talked to him personally because I had to talk to him on behalf of people who wanted to get well. His name is CalChuaChua[1] and he makes people eat compulsively. He's the eater of souls, the spirit of greed.

Because there's good and bad in all things, including in ourselves, we have to choose which trail to follow. The healing trail has nothing to do with the bad. Centuries ago it was recognized that evil forces go along with any sickness. There's always a spiritual reason for any sickness or disturbance of any kind, such as war, which is also a sickness.

Evil spirits have a job to do: they come back to the earth to test people. The entire life process here on this earth is a testing ground. We are continually tested every day of our lives as to which of us is going to live a good life, which of us is strong or weak. Even though you can't see them, both evil and good spirits are always around. There are evil forces working through some people, such as those who are controlled by greed. This country is very badly infested with greed. They are always out to claim someone, and they get people in lots of trouble. Evil spirits cause wars, cause people to be apathetic, to lack compassion. They struggle to control all people, and they don't care what race or who you are. They have respect for no one, and the people who accept them also have respect for no one.

Evil spirits do not necessarily belong on this earth bothering people, but they are invited to do so. The bad ones are invited in if a person goes around thinking bad things and they know that it's wrong. If a person is full of anger and imagines different wrongdoings, that's an invitation. Every thought has an effect.

Evil forces will take advantage of any weakness and any opening, such as people using drugs or alcohol. Of course, people don't have to use those things to invite evil spirits. The bad has a lot of power and can slip into a person when they are wide open or meditating, when their spirit is off guard. I've seen it happen many times. When those things get into a person, they can cause you to think, do, or say things that ordinarily you wouldn't.

Every once in a while you might read in the papers how somebody killed their own child. They say they heard a voice telling them to do it. In these cases it was evil spirits, and they thought it was coming from god. When people go with the evil forces, they could commit any crime in the book and have an excuse for it. They don't think with their hearts and minds, but rather with their mouths, and it comes out wrong. You have to learn to recognize what is you and what is not you. Remember, the evil spirits are always there ready to slip in.

Evil spirits are very strong, and they're always looking for the weak in spirit and mind. The spirits must be welcomed to some degree. Being on the defensive and never examining themselves leaves people wide open and makes them weak. Possession by evil spirits happens. It is our way to help people free themselves from evil spirits, but it has to be at their request. They have to recognize that they're sick, that they wish to get well, that they're thinking the wrong things. When you think the wrong thoughts, eventually you will go crazy. But if people change their thinking and look at natural things, which are always pure, this purity is reflected back into the person. The evil spirits bothering them give up and try to go on to someone else.

Evil spirits can also hang around houses and other buildings where they do not belong. Several houses seemed to slide right off a Chumash sacred peak right after some ceremonies I participated in. The houses were built where they didn't belong. Another time a big boulder shot from a cannon wiped out a roadhouse. It didn't belong there either; the area needed cleansing. You see, before an Indian builds a house or even a wickiup, a medicine man looks over the ground to make sure it's not a burial ground. A medicine man would also know if something should be removed in order to make evil spirits move elsewhere.

I've been in a house not far from Mount Tonopas where a match wouldn't stay lit because there was so much evil in the air. People living in the house couldn't sleep because of strange sounds like people walking through the house all night long, closing doors, talking, and other noise. There was a sound like a little girl out in the brush to one side being raped or murdered all night. I found out later that a bunch of junkies had lived there before and that many crimes had been committed around the place and in the house. It took me three days to clean it up because it was so heavy, and I did so because the people in the house were my friends. This is part of a medicine man's work.

I can tell right away when evil spirits are around. Sometimes you can feel a cold presence that makes you feel chilled all over in the darkness. These spirits might wake you up when you're sleeping. Sometimes I have to call them out and talk to them. It's very dangerous work. You're gonna have to know something about protection if any of you go in for healing. All my doctor friends have the same problems. In many cases they catch the feelings, the sicknesses of their patients, and until they learn how to prevent catching such feelings, they are not immune. Doctors and psychiatrists have the highest rate of alcoholism of any other group. They try to shake off their sickness that way and they can't do it.

A doctor in Elko, an atheist, was my good friend. I had to watch this young man swell up and die. I saw him turning black underneath and I don't think anybody else could see it. I see different colors in and around people, and smell odors that come from them. I can see those things and know what's happening inside a person. But I couldn't talk to my friend because he was an atheist, and he wasn't about to listen to anything spiritual.

I have called evil spirits out of the bodies of people. When the patient would contort and change, you could see the evil leaving them before your eyes. The evil spirits look hideous and they're mean. Each of these evil beings has a name and a look that fits it. I can't make promises to perform a ceremony or doctor someone. When a medicine man makes promises the evil spirits know it as well, and they try to block it so that nothing happens.

There are ways to protect oneself. We medicine men wouldn't be here today if we didn't know something about how to do that. One of the best to start with is to surround yourself with true friends and brothers and sisters. Everyone in this life needs help all the time—standing alone is very hard. You have a choice and people should choose to surround themselves with their mates, families, and friends, leading right on up to the religion or spiritual way of life that fits so that you can have peace of mind and happiness. In this way people become stronger, capable of warding off evil spirits.

It is said that there is a lot of power in our drums. Sometimes we drum the evil spirits right out of people who persist in clinging to them so that they can come back together feeling good. Our songs have power and they are a good way of driving out the evil spirits. We have songs to drive out evil spirits and whatever it is that makes us afraid.

Another necessary way to overcome evil spirits is to continually fight against them in the way you think. Think about something that's good, and you block out the other. What can you think about? Think about flowers, Mother Earth, streams and waterfalls—about nature, which is always pure. You've got to block the bad thoughts in order to bring about healing so that you can become stronger.

You may need sweats and ceremonies in order to heal. Sometimes I like to inhale certain herbal essences. The evil spirits don't like pleasant-smelling odors like eucalyptus and bay leaves. They also don't like the smell of flowers. They like nasty odors like human sewage and chemical stink, rotten eggs, and sulfur. They smell terrible themselves.

Burn incense, cedar, sweetgrass, or sage to purify the place and send the evil spirits away. Incense is very powerful, provided that you make a prayer to clear the air of visitations and make the space pure, that is, free of evil spirits. Don't forget to crack open a door or window to the outside so that the spirits have somewhere to go.

We often put something on our faces before we go to sleep, such as ashes that have been prayed over. The ashes don't do any good unless they've been prayed over. Put a little on the hands, faces, and exposed parts of the body so that the evil spirits don't come and bother you at night.

Another thing I like to see people do if they don't sleep well at night is to hang a mirror at the foot of the bed. Even if you can't see the evil spirits, they can see their own reflections, and their own reflections scare them. They're hideous, and when they see their own reflection, they're afraid and will leave you alone.

If you sense that you are in the presence of an evil spirit, make noise. Scream, holler, tell it to go away or that you don't need it. Sometimes you might have to let out a victory whoop or bawl them out. Make any kind of noise, pray loudly. Usually they'll leave because they're cowards.

Sleep with your feet pointed toward a body of water or a mountain. When there is neither water nor a mountain, sleep with the head toward magnetic north. These positions help you sleep peacefully; evil spirits are not drawn to you.

Evil spirits are attracted to people whose lifestyles are in some way unhealthy. You may have to give up anger, jealousy, aggression, drugs, or alcohol. You have to work against these evil beings and learn how to protect yourself. Nothing can be done permanently to get rid of evil spirits because wrong thinking or a mistake can attract them to you again. Study yourself and try to understand why certain people are plagued with problems.

There is a war going on in the spirit world that's greater than any war that can be conjured up on the earth at this time. This war is between good and evil forces. Not *everything* that happens is meant to be by the Great Spirit.

There are good forces that work through certain people, and they're always around. The Great Spirit's power is in all things that have life. Surround yourself with good people and you'll find that it's catching. You'll pick up good energy.

We must respect the people who have left this physical level of existence. Be very careful not to desecrate their graves or build houses on graveyards. Once a young man from Germany had a Volkswagen full of people with him, and he was on the way to an island in Pyramid Lake. That island is guarded by the spirits of warriors gone on and also by millions of snakes and something else that lives in the water. Nobody belongs in a place like that. But some people will go anywhere because they are pushy and they think they have some kind of immunity. I warned him because he was a very nice, well-mannered young man. He went anyway, and they found his body washed up on the shore of the island. I told the other young people who came back and were feeling bad that the Indian world or the spiritual world is different and can be very dangerous.

At another time I got a letter from San Francisco asking me to hold a ceremony on Mount Tonopas. I had to say no because no Indian can go up there for ceremonies in these times. There's a bunch of junk and houses on the mountain that do not belong there. It's not up to us to clean it up; we didn't put the junk there. Mount Tonopas is a sacred mountain, but it has been desecrated. The fact is that there's a spirit in that mountain and it was known by name.

In the past there were spirits in everything in life, even to the earth itself, and it was called "Earth Mother." I've seen the Earth Mother with tears coming out of her eyes on cliff walls like in Zion Canyon.

The Power of Prayer

Every thought, every word, is a prayer. That's why we train ourselves so powerfully that when we look at someone we have a good thought. Some people tell me they have forgotten how to pray. You'd be surprised how many admit that they don't know how to pray—not like an Indian anyway. I like to teach people how to pray. One of the first things I tell them is to slow down, start to learn, and leave out the trashy parts of the English language.

We well know the power of prayer; it's nothing new to us. But there are different ways of praying and it can be good or bad. It has a force and if people together put out enough energy of that kind, they can do anything.

If you don't take medicine in the right way, if you don't pray in the right way, then you cannot expect to benefit. You might even hurt yourself. Medicine is not to play with. If you get greedy and go too far, then you'll be into an area called witchcraft, and that would be the start of your own wrongdoing and your own end. Every thought, twenty-four hours a day, is a prayer. That's what has to guide our lives.

People use the wrong language, the "I want." Great Spirit doesn't give a damn about what you or any of us wants. The Great Spirit is interested in what's good for you and what you could benefit from, or what makes you healthy and feel good. We have to approach Great Spirit's power in a humble way. We can't go there demanding or with a demanding attitude. We

Indians usually put in our prayers, "if it's meant to be." We like to have a little leeway there because we might ask for something that we're not entitled to. It's good if we pray for nature, animals, rocks, and mountains, and the water. That's the way to orient prayers and thinking so that they can be effective and acceptable to the Great Spirit.

You can make a prayer wherever you are, and it doesn't have to be out loud. You can pray anytime day or night. I go to sleep praying at night, and I wake up in the morning praying. If I wake up in the night, I pray myself back to sleep, and I don't think I'm any kind of exception. A person can attain spiritual awareness through prayer, fasting, and the right kind of meditation. I do not agree with crutches of any kind, including drugs or alcohol, to attain spiritual awareness.

The Great Spirit wants you to stand up when you pray like we do. Stand up and be proud. Be proud to be alive, proud for your life on this Mother Earth, and thankful at the same time, rather than bowing down like a slave. We don't have regimented prayers, routines, or anything like that. But we do pray all the time for our brothers and sisters, even if it appears that we are doing nothing or being intimidated. We have ceremonies where we pray for all our brothers and sisters around the world—spiritual brothers and sisters, that is. We say "all my relations" in our prayers, and we're not merely talking about our blood relations. We're talking about all spiritual people around the world.

I'd like to see people learn how to pray like the old-time Indians, with proper respect and regard for all the life forces that the Great Spirit has placed here, including oneself. Our prayers are sometimes long, but most are short. Sometimes we might say to "all our relations" and then go over and put tobacco on the fire. We don't pray for our enemies because they already have too much power. We turn our backs, try to forget about them. All people should be thinking about regard for life forces, not about enemies. Enemies will soon fade away, change, or whatever is meant to be. We should pray more for peace. You can pray that politicians and other people will change their ways and reverse their thinking. Pray for the Mother Earth.

Watch your thinking. In the camp where I was raised I saw little children run screaming when some foreigner arrived to steal the children, ship them off to boarding schools, and the children would never see their families again. But the children would know; they have a way of knowing, just like the wild animals. Many of our people still have what you might call intuition. Originally all peoples had that ability to sense danger.

Thoughts are powerful. If you think something long enough, it comes into being. The ancient people knew this, and they had clear minds. Children's minds are clear when they are born, and they stay that way until they are corrupted. Modern people do not have the clear minds and thinking capacity of the people of ancient civilizations. Modern people seem to have become regimented to the extent that they can't think for themselves. Ancient man had a clear mind and could out-think modern man ten to one. Their minds were not cluttered up with trash, aggression, and filth. The human brain is only so big: if it's already cluttered up with bad things, then there isn't the capacity left for clear thinking. When people's minds are filled with such things, they will make mistakes in whatever they do, create wasteful things, or spend themselves in creating something for war or making themselves a million dollars.

Some of the people who have come to me complained that

they can't control their thinking. In some cases, their minds are messed up, already damaged by drugs or alcohol. In other cases, the poisons they have ingested in their food and water and by breathing had affected their thinking and weakened them. That's a pitiful condition to be in. But I tell them they can control their thinking if they try; I can teach them if they keep their mouths shut, slow down, and listen.

If people practice thinking good things, after a while it gets to be a habit. You might develop enough power so that you can think of anything you want to at any time. Minds should be exercised like any other muscle, and should not be blanked or dulled in any way. The Great Spirit gave people brains and he wants them to use their brains. When your arm is in a cast too long it could become atrophied and stiff. It's the same way with brain power. We're supposed to strengthen our minds as we go along every day, every minute.

Some people suffer a great deal when they accept the bad; they become possessed. This is why people should learn to control their thinking. Depression and unhappiness are a sickness that people suffer from when they get self-centered and sorry for themselves. Any little thing comes along gets magnified and multiplies, until the next thing you know they aren't good for anything. If you permit yourself to engage in wrong thinking, you may be on the way to a mental institution or prison.

I remember a time when I had a lot of bad luck, but I learned that I had no time to waste with worry about myself. I think that might have been the start of my real spiritual development. I was born to be a medicine man, but actually I didn't make a great deal of progress until I got over my own ego and my own worries and learned not to let those things bother me too much. A great many problems are created in one's own mind. Mental control and stability can be attained through proper diet, fasting, meditation, and ceremonies.

You can hurt someone if you're not careful about your thinking. If you look at someone with a hostile thought, a bad thought, you can make that person sick. You can make yourself sick because your own reflection will come back to you. If you hurt someone even with a thought, you will pay for it.

If we put out good energy with our thoughts, it comes back to us multiplied by seven, and it travels in a circle left to right. If we make medicine in a bad way, such as a bad thought causing someone trouble or pain, it travels from left to right and comes back to the one that did it multiplied by seven. This is the Law of the Spirit.

We should be very careful and correct in our thinking. If enough people get to thinking that they can't stop what they're doing or change their lifestyle or their thinking, if a lot of people get to thinking we're going to have a war because there is nothing we can do about it, we are going to get ourselves blown right off the face of the earth. But if we turn that number seven around and start thinking of good things, the bad ones will cease to be.

That's why, regardless of what anyone else may think of us, we try first to have good thoughts. When we meet someone, even an enemy, the first thought has to be a good thought or a healing thought. If I catch myself having a bad thought, I look at a green plant or a little baby or an animal. To look at anything like that and have a bad thought is an impossibility for me, because they're all beautiful. Things like that clear my thoughts real quick, and I bring myself back into order. When you start to think something that's bad, all you have to do is look at the clouds or the trees, or look at the children playing. That's the way you remove bad thinking, and make room for the good forces to come in, the ones that enable you to be a powerful healer. Once you've rid your mind of bad thinking, if you think of something strongly enough, it will come into being.

In other words, you have to exercise your thinking and purify the mind so that you can heal. You can make bones come together, even to the point where you might not need an x-ray machine or all those laboratory tests. You can heal yourself to the point that you can see into a sick person—a certain color in a certain spot—or smell a powerful odor; in this way you recognize the type of sickness. You can heal yourself from being paranoid or uptight, or from having bad thoughts. You have to actually see it happening. If the mind is clear enough, anybody can do it. Call on the power of the Great Spirit; that's the way it's done.

I like to use my energy and my thoughts in a way that is beneficial to everyone in my presence. I like to see those things happen inside the body. But I also like to apply it to the forest, to nature, even the animals and the birds. If you want to understand the oneness of all things, you should start thinking of yourself as with nature, with other human beings and other spiritual people throughout the world, and even the universe. If you think of it in that order so that when you go out and look at the stars, the sky, the moon at night, that you would recognize all these things as part of one and the same thing as yourselves.

If enough people learn how to pray, then a lot of the bad things in the prophecies don't have to happen. The pattern of things taking us into destruction could be changed. You might reach a point where you don't hate anybody or think about making war on anybody. That's when you really start to get well, and your children will grow up to be better people. And if you don't find the answers to how to clean up the air, the water, the earth, there will be a time when your children would because they'd grow up to be a peaceful people. They would grow up to be clear thinkers, and they could even learn five times faster in school than they would ordinarily.

If enough of you Thunder People get together and really learn how to pray, you could even pray the smog away, or ask that it be cleaned up, and it would be. There's a lot of power in prayer. Don't underestimate your own power to do good.

Meditation

We believe in meditation, but it must always have a purpose. You can't benefit from meditation unless it has a purpose, such as benefiting yourself and possibly someone else, when you get on a level where you can do that. I've seen some of the old-timers sit out in the sunshine or with their back to a tree. They knew they could draw energy for their backs when they hurt from the tree or from the Mother Earth where they'd be sitting. But they were meditating about drawing that energy into them. They didn't think about foolishness and they didn't vacate their minds.

There are good and bad ways of meditating, as there is good and bad in all things. I've seen some people in terrible shape who have been meditating. I remember a fourteen-year-old boy who visited our camp, and every time he sat down he would go into meditation. He'd slip into meditation without wanting to because he'd been trained wrong. I've straightened out a number of these types of people, and it makes me angry to have to straighten out what somebody else messed up.

Meditation requires guidance or someone to tell you how to protect yourself. When you start stepping into things that exist in the other world, you might not come out. You're deal-ing with powerful forces; they are real and they can harm you or you can hurt someone else. There are good and bad spirits, and the bad ones can slip in and cause you to think something wrong at a certain time when you take medicine or meditate.

I don't like to see people inexperienced in the spiritual world who can't control their thinking getting into things where they can hurt themselves. Don't overdo meditation and don't do it because it's trendy. Keep in mind that you're med-itating for some objective purpose that the Great Spirit ap-proves of. Don't blank your mind and let the evil spirits come in. The Great Spirit gave us a brain and he wants us to use it, not knock it out with drugs, alcohol, or meditation. The way I advise people to meditate is to put the trash of civilization out of the mind, but keep the mind active with good thoughts.

If you ever attend a healing session, don't go with a blank mind and don't meditate with a blank mind. Be yourself and let the Great Spirit be your guide. In other words, when I'm doing a healing, I start out thinking about what's needed and seeing into the person. If it is a broken bone, I like to see the bones coming together, and I do see them. Sometimes I see people long distance. I might see a big tumor inside their body or something like that just vanishing and going away. That is meditation in its highest form.

Dreams and Prophecy

In the old days every tribe had its medicine people, and pro-phets or seers. White society calls them psychics, and we say seers. I like to have a seer around me. Seers can tell me things that help me avoid a bad situation or change it completely for the good. Seers work with the Great Spirit's power too. They try to help people deal with the daily problems of their lives.

These abilities are not something we exercise because we simply want to. We listen to everyone, even the young ones. We listen to dreams for guidance. We put it together and some of us interpret. All prophecy is subject to change. I've told you that if people put their hearts and minds together the bad things wouldn't have to happen. Well, it's the same way with your own life. If you know what's coming at you, you have the power within yourself to change it. You can change it in many different ways, including with a prayer. You can go around it to avoid it. So keep in mind when you have a reading and if something isn't exactly the way you want it, or the way you think it ought to be, just remember that it doesn't have to be that way.

Dreams are the reality. Our physical bodies are here only for a short time and the reality of the spiritual in the dream as we refer to it is permanent. So the dreams represent the past, the present, or the future, or are put together as one. Dreams and visions are one and the same thing. Both come from the same places and they come sometimes as warnings, and sometimes as guidance. They should always be paid attention to. We put them to use in our daily lives to avoid bad things or accidents. We exchange our knowledge, our dreams, and our prophecies so that we are guided by them for our own future good and that of our people. That's part of our job of being here on this Mother Earth.

Visiting Hell

I've been where evil spirits go. Every true medicine person has been there too. It's part of the training to go there and learn how it is and how to cope with those things, but not to stay. It's just a learning place and then no longer needed. I have known some bad Indians who had killed people in warfare or drinking arguments, so I got to wondering where these people go. I used to think hell was an Indian reservation until after this experience.

I doctored myself using two eagle plumes from under the tail of an eagle. I'm not going to tell you what else I did to fix myself because some amateur might try to copy me and get into trouble. Before the night passed I found myself in a large canyon with steep cliffs on all sides. I didn't know where I was because time and space had changed so quickly. Even so, I didn't like the vibes and started looking up to see how to climb out of there.

At the top of the cliffs were evil spirits with big round eyes that never blinked. These demons or evil spirits were everywhere and looked right at me. We didn't have to talk. I knew that they would stomp on my hands or feet if I got to the top of the cliffs and make me fall down to the bottom again. I had to think about this situation and where I was; I had forgotten all about fixing myself to visit this place. I decided to take a walk, and soon I saw this cute little bar with neon signs around the door far in the distance, so I started walking in that direction. Along the way I passed within fifty yards of where some beautiful girls were dancing. They were all young, dressed in miniskirts, but a somewhat older woman seemed to be in charge of these girls. Since I was raised as an Indian with Indian manners, I merely looked but walked on by until I got to the bar that was built in the side of a cliff. It had a big brown oak door with a brass handle.

When my spirit guide told me that there was no one inside

and nothing to drink, I argued. I told him that I would not drink more than three beers and that maybe the bartender or a barfly could tell me where I was or how to get out. My spirit guide told me to go ahead and open the door. There was nothing but rock behind the door. My spirit guide was right after all.

I walked back toward the fire where the girls were dancing, and stopped at the edge of the fire's light. That is when the woman, the clan mother of these girls, came out to where I was standing. I knew instantly that she was going to be my future wife. This girl, Spotted Fawn, was very polite and asked me if there was something they could do to assist me. I said yes, that I think I didn't like it here, and that I wanted to get out. So she went into a huddle with the other girls and they said that they would help me.

They took me to an old trail that went up the side of the cliff that hadn't been used in a long time. So I had an all-girl army. While walking to the trail with the girl army, I did mention that she (my future wife) had some very good-looking girls and she said, "Yes, but no sex."

At that point I knew I really was in hell and that I wanted out. My future wife also instructed me and the girls to pick up big rocks on the trail to hurl at the evil spirits. The evil spirits would cry out something like "Don't do that," or "That hurts," and then disappear.

In this hell where the bad Indians go, there was no one burning forever and ever. It was not that gruesome, but there was no vegetation, no sage, no grass, no trees, nothing alive. There were no children, no rain. Everything was in darkness except for the neon sign of the bar and the fire where the girls were dancing. Everything else was dark. There were no white people. It seems they had gone to their own kind of hell, which is a different place entirely.

Karma

Once I read in the Old Testament that you reap what you sow, and the sins of the father are vested on the children until the seventh generation. The number seven is in the Old Testament and in all ancient teachings, and there is a payment to make to the seventh generation. So you're stuck with it whether you like it or not. The sons of the father suffer for the sins of the father until the seventh generation.

We're supposed to live in peace and brotherhood. According to one of our prophecies, the descendants of the treaty breakers will have to live by those treaties. When you give your word there is no way to get away from it until the spell is broken, until some kind of atonement is made to break that spell. The spell is the curse of the treaty breakers, the wrongdoers who saturated the whole land with the blood of the Indians.

How is the spell broken? I'll try to tell you in as few words as possible and in plain English. In the first place, don't sit in church on Sunday and pray about it unless you mean it. The only way to mean it is to do something about it. Some people say that they had nothing to do with broken treaties and mayhem, that they can't be held responsible for their heritage. But like it or not, it's up to you to break the spell or you are going to suffer. People who go to church on Sundays or learn to meditate, and who don't give a damn about the Indians, or perhaps their own neighbors down the street or their relations, think they're okay. Well, I have a surprise for them.

This thing about karma is that, good or bad, it comes back to us and is compounded by seven. There's no escaping karma. If you've done something wrong, there is no escape from making atonement or reparations. The Great Spirit doesn't make exceptions for anybody. No person, no nation can ever get away from it; no one is immune. It's already been added up and counted. Entire nations are sick, suffering from a great deal of misfortune. They can't blame it on anybody else; it's their own karma.

We are all part of the whole. There is a payment for anyone who gets hurts unnecessarily, even an animal, a bird, or an ant. There has to be a payment for any type of destruction, whether it's the trees or the mountains. There must be a payment, and it will be multiplied by seven when it comes back to the starting point.

Whatever you put out, good or bad, it's gonna come back. That's why a lot of people get sick. That's why a lot of people have car wrecks and get hurt. A person gets sick because they have done something to deserve it. In our prayers, we say "if it's meant to be," because some people's time is gone or they might be paying for karma; some people are supposed to die and their karma can go back seven generations.

Some people don't think karma is fair. I didn't make that rule and neither did you, but the number seven is in all ancient teachings and all magic and medicine. Whatever you have coming to you, that's what you're going to get, not what you want. That's the way it is all through life, which is a test for each and every one of us.

Change your thinking to become stronger and more honest. I know many who are doing just that—they are helping the American Indian, helping each other, helping their parents or their elders. We keep ourselves on a high spiritual level, and you only attain this level through compassion for each other.

Death and Reincarnation

A few years ago some elderly people in Oakland called me to talk to them, and they wanted me to talk about the meaning of death. I'd rather talk about the things of beauty and the meaning of life because so many people have never lived, have never been alive. And that's what I told them.

After the meeting the elderly gentleman who had set up the meeting was shaking, and he said that I had scared the living bejeebers out of those old people. I had told them the truth. They had seen their families split up, and some of them were trying to figure out ways of taking their money with them. My words shocked them. I like to shock people: sometimes it wakes them up and brings them to life, and that's what they needed to come awake.

The Great Spirit determines whether we live or die. Actually there is no death. There's only a crossing over. Our knowledge is about the same as all the other ancient religions and peoples. We are not in conflict with any religions that are true. Every life is lived according to the way we lived the previous one. The next life is an extension of how we lived this life. Ordinarily we fulfill twelve lifetimes. Each time we are supposed to go to a higher plane. Say that someone hated black people all his or her life or had black slaves. In the next life that person would be born as a black person and he'll go through the same trials and tribulations that a black person did in his previous life. In other words, it comes back to us, whatever we put out.

After we die, we could go to many different places rather than only one or two, according to what we qualify for. We are supposed to elevate ourselves to higher levels every day. Every new day is supposed to be lived better than the day before, and the things of yesterday should be put in the past. Every year of our lives in each lifetime we are supposed to go to a higher level so that eventually we don't have to come back. This physical life plane is a learning place and will no longer be needed after that.

In the Indian way, after twelve lives when we die we are granted thirty days to visit our old friends and relations. Then two warriors come to guide us to the Happy Hunting Ground. All real medicine people have to go to those places, so I know where I'm going. I don't have to come back, even though I've only had three lives; this is common with medicine people.

A person goes to a higher level in each life, unless he commits suicide or murder, even in warfare. There is no excuse for suicide or murder. If one of these happens, we have to suffer, and we might go back to a lower plane, such as being reborn as a worm or a coyote. Then we have to work our way all the way back up, or spend some time in a special school or in Indian hell where bad Indians go, which is different from the white man's hell.

All people have jobs to do in life. We're not supposed to throw our lives away by committing suicide or unconsciously committing suicide by taking drugs or alcohol and other things that destroy our minds and bodies. We have to make the best of our lives by helping someone else—that's the job that we're supposed to be doing at all times.

Our bodies are imperfect and wear out sometimes these days after only a very short time through accidents, abuse, the wrong kind of living, and by the chemicals we get in food, water, and the air. Our bodies are not "real" because they are only temporary. But the spirit lives on and on. And so it is we create our own hell and our own heaven, starting right here.

The Happy Hunting Ground

There is no similarity between our spiritual way of life and modern American society. The difference is like the day and the night. Although I never got an answer, many times I asked my minister friends, "When you get to the pearly gates and Saint Peter holds out that plate, what are you gonna put in it? You're gonna have to buy your way in because you bought your way through this life. That dollar became your god and so when you get over there, how do you think it's going to be any different? The next life has to be an extension of this life and the way you have lived this life. So what are you going to put in the plate that has value?"

I know where I'm going, and I don't need a missionary to tell me. I've been there many times when I had died or rather been left for dead. When we traditional Indians cross over, two warriors come to guide us. When we get there, there is a large canyon to cross. If we are not qualified, the canyon does not close up and it is too wide to jump. Human beings cannot fly like a bird or an angel in this place; so if we aren't qualified we must come back and maybe start life all over again. If we are qualified, the canyon closes up and we walk over to the Happy Hunting Ground.

On one of my visits my guide for the day was waiting for me. He seemed to be making a flute. He looked up and smiled and motioned for me to come over. I followed him to the village. Many children were playing and running and laughing, so I know that with so many children they do have sex in the Happy Hunting Ground. What would heaven be without children running, playing, and laughing?

Women with long hair in long buckskin dresses were cooking and singing Indian songs while they worked. Everyone looked healthy, and seemed happy and well fed. There was no disease, no sickness. There was no pollution anywhere, even in their thinking. There wasn't a lot of speaking out loud. It seemed that we were so close it was not necessary to talk. No thoughts of war, greed, gold, or money; no war, no taxes. We were at peace, not only with each other, but also with everything around us, including all living things and all two- and four-legged, and winged creatures.

The young man who was my guide that day took me through the camp so I was able to see that the houses were constructed out of willows like some of our wickiups. Some of these were huge with many rooms but they were also kind of out in the open. Some places were covered with buffalo hides to keep the rain out of the cooking and to give shade from the sun. The climate was like springtime, cool and not hot. There was knee-deep grass and rich soil. Far in the distance about a mile away I could see a long line of buffalo strung out for several miles as far as the eye could see.

There were no cares, no worries, no stress. It was beautiful, and beautiful Indian music was playing. One thing I did notice was that there were only Indians. But I believe that good people of all kinds who have not lied, broken treaties, or killed even in warfare, and who had been kind to Indians will be allowed in. There will never be any of the treaty breakers or those who made war on the Native Americans or other Native peoples in the Happy Hunting Ground. Everyone will be purified, in body as well as spirit. No disease will be brought into the Happy Hunting Ground. Then they will take on a new spiritual body of a healthy Indian with a reddish brown color. They will look the same as American Indians. That's where I'll be going when my time is up in this life. I have no desire to go anywhere else.

The Seven Laws of the Great Spirit

We have seven laws to guide us and advise us in our daily lives. The whites have ten called "commandments," another example of English as military language, and it doesn't sound good in song. Our languages are soft and musical, but we do the best we can to make things clear and to educate people in English.

We were given the code, the seven laws, by the Great Spirit himself a long time ago. An old Indian man who's been gone for many years gave it to me a long time ago. I'd almost forgotten it, but then as I thought about it, it came back to me slowly but surely.

Number one is respect for proper authority. Our Native way of life teaches us respect for grandparents, chiefs, medicine people, and for Grandmother Moon, Mother Earth, and everything that has life. We are a law abiding people; I've sat on a few of our courts. In a small case there would be one judge reaching agreement with both parties in the contest. In a big case like murder or rape, three judges would reach agreement with both parties in contest. There was no appeal except going to the chief's council, but because everything started out with an agreement for justice, the appeal didn't usually do any good because the intent was to avoid having to put up with somebody wanting to overrule or destroy their own.

Number two is to preserve and promote the beauties of nature. I don't believe there is anything like this in the books of Christians, Buddhists, or Muslims, but there should be.

Number three is to judge with kindness and wisdom. The white man's Bible tells you not to judge. Our law is to judge but with kindness and wisdom. Even a little baby starts to judge when it's born about whether it's hungry or wants a diaper change, and it will let you know. Great Spirit gave us a brain to use to exercise good judgment, whether it's about a job or a relationship. We should use judgment in our daily lives so that we are not gullible or taken advantage of.

Number four is moderation in all things. We say that if it helps, it is good. We're not told don't do this or don't do that, but rather to exercise moderation, and that covers a lot. We don't want to be extremists, and this takes us out of the category of being fanatics.

Number five is to play fair in the game of life. It is not fair to take advantage of old people, women, or children. It is not fair to invade someone else's land or home and demand that they fight you for it. Beating up your neighbors is not fair. Filling food with preservatives and drinking water with chemicals is not fair.

Number six is that a person's word of honor is sacred. The United States government doesn't make treaties with counties or states, only with sovereign nations. There were three hundred and ninety-seven treaties in the United States with Indians. All were broken by the government. We are asking these people to be honorable, to stop lying and stealing and breaking treaties. We have to be honorable ourselves if we wish for others to be honest. We have always kept our word, kept our treaties, because it was in our teachings.

Number seven is respect for differences, the basis of Indian teachings. Everything we do in our way of life has to be based on respect for other people and all living things. The Great Spirit made people of different colors like flowers. There are red flowers, white flowers, black flowers, and yellow flowers. These flowers all make us feel good when we look at them, and this is the way it is supposed to be when we walk among other people—we should walk with courtesy and respect, and never with aggression or lies because of their color or nationality. We should only think of beautiful things when we look at other people.

People are not all the same. Maybe someday we will be, but in any event that's the white man's propaganda. Don't believe it. The Creator made us in different colors, different nationalities, and that is the way he intended us to be. The same force put all of us here; all of us are supposed to live and bloom just like the flowers. We know that we all belong here in all our differences, and that we must get along with each other. It would be mighty boring if everyone looked alike.

Restoring the Circle

People all over the world are looking for a spiritual way of life. I don't claim that I know all the answers, but I know a few. No one but a missionary or dictator claims to knows all the answers.

Finding the answers in traveling the spiritual way of life is a sorting out process. It is said that we find each other, people of good heart, as we travel. When we run into the others, those not of good heart, we don't want controversy or struggle—we don't want anything to do with them. Instead the idea is to put our minds together and through the Spirit we can be as one.

The time will come when we can put all our minds together as one in a powerful way of healing. When I speak of
healing I'm not talking about healing only people, but also the
plants, nature, and Mother Earth and everything that has life.
We will bring all into a circle so that the circle shall not be
broken.

Not everyone is meant to be a medicine person or a healer,
but anyone can be a spiritual person. A warrior for peace can
be a man or a woman who may someday join with us in this
circle of peace. Then these circles will join together and spread
around the world again. We Indian people want to come as
friends and brothers so we can come together in that kind of
way and as equals. We want other cultures to accept us as we
accept those who are respectful. Medicine men, priests, and
rabbis can advise, but it's up to individual people to right any
wrongs they or their governments have committed.

It is good to be alive and to see others come alive. That's
spiritual. When I see your eyes sparkle, when I see you look like
an eagle, and I see that you understand me and I understand
you—that is spiritual. I'd like to see you on a high enough level
that we can get along and recognize each other, wherever it is
that we meet again.

All I'm asking is that you make a good prayer. Don't forget
to pray for the animals, the birds, the plant life, the rocks, and
the mountains so that you may walk a long beauty trail and
into the land of the Great Mystery. And don't forget me. My
friends and my brothers, whatever race you are, whoever you
are, wherever you are, I never want you to forget me for one
minute, and the best way not to forget me is to learn to live

with each other. Walk with the Grandfather Great Spirit, and the knowledge that I love all of you. *Aho.*

NOTE

1. Typically, only medicine people and elders know the personal names of spirits, both good and evil. To know a spirit's name is to have power. Rolling Thunder "called the spirit out" from people by calling the spirit's name. He specifically mentions CalChuaChua because the materialism and greed in non-Indian society is evidence of how badly infested the world is by this spirit.

Photographs